THE FERN BOOK

THE FERN BOOK

Text and Prints by
Mabel Crittenden

CELESTIAL ARTS
Millbrae, California

To Gerda Isenberg,
who shares her love of ferns

Cover illustration and design by Betsy Bruno

Copyright © 1978 by Mabel Crittenden
Celestial Arts
231 Adrian Road
Millbrae, California 94030

First Printing, February 1978
Made in the United States of America

Library of Congress Cataloging in Publication Data

Crittenden, Mabel, 1917-
    The fern book.

    Bibliography: p.
    Includes index.
    1.   Ferns, Ornamental,   1.   Title.
SB429.C74   635.9'37'31   77-90021
ISBN 0-89087-227-9

1   2   3   4   5   6   7 — 84   83   82   81   80   79   78

Contents

FERNS

TENDER to SEMI-TENDER: *Special Maidenhairs*, 31; *Dwarf Mother Fern*, 34; *Bird's Nest Fern*, 35; *Rabbit's Foot*, 36; *Hand Fern*, 38; *Boston Fern*, 39; *Maidenhair Cliff Brake*, 43; *Green Cliff Brake*, 44; *Hare's Foot Fern*, 45; *Victorian Brake*, 46; *Downy Wood Fern*, 47.

SEMI-TENDER to SEMI-HARDY: *Delta Maidenhair*, 49; *Rosy Maidenhair*, 50; *Mother Fern*, 51; *Hammock Fern*, 53; *Squirrel's Foot Fern*, 54; *Lace Fern*, 55, *Southern Sword Fern*, 57; *Common Sword Fern*, 58; *Australian Cliff Brake*, 59; *Button Fern*, 60; *Gold Back Fern*, 61; *Staghorn Fern*, 63; *California Polypody*, 65; Table Fern, 66; *Silver Brake*, 72; *Pteris dentata*, 73; *Ladder Brake Fern*, 74; *Australian Brake*, 75; *Leather Fern*, 76; Tree Ferns, 78.

SEMI-HARDY to HARDY: *Southern Maidenhair*, 83; *Holly Fern*, 85; *Rocheford Holly Fern*, 87; *Coastal Wood Fern*, 88; *Shaggy Shield Fern*, 89; *Dwarf Leather-Leaf Fern*, 90, *Tassel Fern*, 92.

HARDY to VERY HARDY: *Five-Finger Fern*, 93; Asparagus Ferns, 94; *Lady Fern*, 97; *Japanese Painted Fern*, 99; *Deer Tongue*, 100; *Covelle's Lip Fern*, 101; *Autumn Fern*, 103; *Male Fern*, 104; *Evergreen Shield Fern*, 105; *Spinulose Woodfern*, 106; *Sensitive Fern*, 108; *Royal Fern*, 109; *Hart's Tongue*, 111; *California Gold Fern*, 112; *Christmas Fern*, 113; *Western Sword Fern*, 114; *Soft Shield Fern*, 116; *Bracken*, 118; Chain Ferns, 120.

Ferns—A Comparative List

Key to Abbreviations

Col. 2 — T = Tender
ST = Semi-Tender
SH = Semi-Hardy
H = Hardy
VH = Very Hardy

Col. 3 — VM = Very Moist
M = Moist
M/D = Moist/Dry
D = Dry

Col. 5 — L = Low
M = Medium
H = High
SS = Some Sun

Col. 12 — * = Easy
** = Very Easy

	Terrarium	Tenderness/Hardiness	Moisture Required	Color	Light Required	Basket	Fertilize every 2 weeks	Fertilize once monthly	Produces Fernlets	Deciduous/Evergreen	Needs Lime	Easy
Adiantum capillus–veneris Southern Maidenhair		SH–H	M		M		*			E+	*	*
A. capillus–veneris cv Imbricatus		ST–SH	M		L–M		*			E	*	
A. hispidulum Rosy Maidenhair	*	ST–SH	M	*	L–M		*			E	*	**
A. pedatum Five Finger		H	M		L–M	*	*			E	*	**
A. raddianum Delta Maidenhair		ST	M		L–M		*			E	*	
A. raddianum cv Pacific Maid		ST–SH	M		L–M	*	*			E	*	
A. raddianum cv Triumph		ST	M		L–M	*	*			E	*	
Asparagus densiflorus cv Myeri		H	M		M		*			E		*
A. densiflorus cv Sprengerii		H	M		H–SS	*	*			*		*
A. setaceus		H	M		H		*			E		*
Asplenium bulbiferum Mother Fern		ST–SH	M		L	*	*		*	E		**
A. daucifolium Dwarf Mother Fern	*	ST	M		L		*		*	E		
A. nidus Bird's Nest Fern		ST–SH	M		L–M			*		E		**
Athyrium filix–femina Lady Fern		H	M		M–SS			*		D		**
A. niponicum cv Pictum Japanese Painted		H	M/D	*	M–H			*		D		
Blechnum occidentale Hammock Fern	*	ST–SH	M/D	*	H			*		E	*	*
B. spicant Deer's Tongue		H	M		L			*		E		*
Cheilanthes covellei Lip Fern		H	D		H			*		E		
Cibotium glaucum Hawaiian Tree Fern		ST	M		H			*		E		

Name												
C. schiedei — Mexican Tree Fern		ST	M/D		M			*		E		
Cyrtomium falcatum — Holly Fern		SH–H	M/D		M		*			E		**
C. falcatum cv Rochefordianum		SH–H	M/D		M		*			E		
Davallia fejeensis — Rabbit's Foot	*	T	M/D		L–H	*	*			E		**
D. trichomanoides — Squirrel's Foot	*	ST–SH	M/D		L–H	*	*			E		**
Dicksonia antarctica — New Zealand Tree Fern		ST–SH	M		H			*		E		
Doryopteris pedata var palmata — Hand Fern	*	T	M		M			*	*	E		
Dryopteris arguta — Coastal Wood Fern		SH–H	D		L–M			*		E		*
D. atrata — Shaggy Shield Fern		SH–H	M/D		M			*		E		*
D. erythrosa — Autumn Fern		H	M	*	L			*		E		*
D. filix-mas — Male Fern		H	M		L			*		D/E		*
D. intermedia — Evergreen Shield Fern		VH	M		M–SS			*		E		
D. spinulosa — Spinulose Fern		H⁻	M		L			*		E±		*
Humata tyermannii — Bear's Foot		SH	M/D		H–M	*	*			E		*
Microlepia strigosa — Lace Fern		ST–SH	M/D		H			*		E		*
Nephrolepis cordifolia — Tuber Sword Fern		ST–SH	M/D		L–H			*		E		*
N. exaltata — Common Sword		ST	M/D		L–H			*	*	E		*
N. exaltata var bostoniensis — Boston Fern		T	M/D		L–H	*	*		*	E		**
N. exaltata compacta — Dwarf Boston		T	M/D		L–H		*		*	E		
N. exaltata cv Florida Ruffles		T	M/D		L–H		*		*	E		
N. exaltata cv Fluffy Ruffles		T	M/D		L–H		*		*	E		
N. exaltata cv Trevillian		T	M/D		L–H	*	*		*	E		
Onoclea sensibilis — Sensitive Fern		H	VM		H–SS			*		D		*
Osmunda regalis — Royal Fern		VH	VM		L			*		D		
Pellaea falcata — Australian Cliff Brake		ST–SH	M/D		H	*	*			E	*	
P. rotundifolia — Button Fern	*	SH	M/D		H	*	*			E	*	*
P. viridis var macrophyllum	*	ST	M/D		H	*				E+	*	
P. viridis var viridis — Green Cliff Brake	*	ST	M/D		H	*				E+	*	
Phyllitis scolopendrium — Hart's Tongue		H	M		L		*			E	*	*
Pityrogramma hybrida — Goldback Fern		ST SH	M/D	*	H		*			D+		
P. triangularis — California Goldback		H	D	*	H			*		D		

Platycerium bifurcatum Staghorn		ST	M/D		H	*		*	*	E		
Polypodium aureum var areolatum		T–ST	M	*	H	*		*		E		**
P. californicum California Polypody		ST–SH	M		L			*		D		*
Polystichum acrostichoides Christmas Fern		H	M		L			*		E	*	**
P. munitum Western Sword Fern		H	M		L			*		E		**
P. polyblepharum Tassel Fern		SH–H	M/D		M–H			*		E		*
P. setiferum Soft Shield		H	M/D		M			*		E		**
P. tsus-simense Tsusima Holly Fern	*	SH–H	M/D		L–M			*		E		*
Pteridium aquilinum		H	M/D		H					D		**
Pteris argyraea Silver Brake		ST–SH	M	*	H			*		E		**
Pteris cretica cv Albo—lineata Variegated Table Fern	*	SH	M	*	M–H			*		E		*
P. cretica cv Ouvrardii	*	SH	M–D		H			*		E		**
P. cretica cv Parkeri Parker Table Fern	*	SH	M		M			*		E		*
P. cretica cv Rivertoniana Lacy Table Fern	*	SH	M		M			*		E		*
P. cretica cv Wilsonii Fan Table Fern		ST	M		M			*		E		*
P. cretica cv Wimsettii	*	ST	M		M			*		E		*
P. dentata		ST–SH	M		M			*		E		*
P. ensiformis var Victoriae	*	ST	M	*	M			*		E		**
P. tremula Australian Brake		ST–SH	M		M–H			*		E		**
P. vittata Ladder Fern		ST–SH	M		M–H	*				E		*
Rumohra adiantiformis Leather Fern		ST–SH	M/D		M–H		*			E		**
Sphaeropteris cooperi Australian Tree Fern		ST–SH	M/D		H			*		E		*
Thelypteris dentata Downy Wood Fern		ST	M		M			*		D±		*
Woodwardia fimbriata Giant Chain Fern		H	M		H			*		D		*
W. orientalis Oriental Chain Fern		H	M		H				*	D		*
W. radicans European Chain Fern		H	M		H				*	E		*
W. Virginica Virginia Chain Fern		H	VM		H–SS					D		

Introduction

Ferns can be fantastic houseplants, lovely as patio or entry plants, and great in gardens almost anywhere.

As houseplants they are really special since houseplants should be chosen for their interesting foliage, form, color and texture, not particularly for their flowers, for very few plants really bloom well indoors. Since ferns don't bloom anyway, you can choose ferns with shiny, broad fronds like Bird's Nest *(Asplenium nidus)* to contrast with finely divided dark green ones like the Fiji Davallia. Or grow Rosy Maidenhairs *(Adiantum hispidulum)* and Hammock Ferns *(Blechnum occidentale)* for color, or the Button Fern *(Pellaea rotundifolia)* with its small, round, dark green leaves to contrast with the feathery, long, light green fronds of a Boston Fern. Ferns can grow in a terrarium, a pot, along a windowsill, or fill a corner with a lush hanging container. Most ferns do not like strong light, so house conditions are often ideal.

As outside plants, they are real additions, too, for they come in a variety of sizes, shapes, and textures to serve as focal points or as backgrounds. Some are evergreen to enhance the area all year; others are deciduous and provide interest from the time their curled croziers appear till they die down in late fall.

There are *tender ferns* (T) which need nighttime temperatures no lower than 60°F, and *semitender* (ST) ferns preferring temperatures not lower than 45°F to 50°F, while the *semihardy* (SH) ferns can stand nights almost to freezing. Then there are *hardy* (H) ferns which can live though temperatures go to 10°F, and the *very hardy* (VH) ferns which can stand long periods of very cold weather—to minus 25°F.

The leaves of ferns are called *fronds.* These can be very simple (as the Bird's Nest), once-divided or one-pinnate like the Sword or Christmas Fern in which the frond is divided into leaflets called *pinnae.* Or two-pinnate, when the pinna is divided to the midrib, making subleaflets called *pinnules.* Or three-pinnate, when those pinnules are divided to their midrib—as in the *Davallias* or the Mother Ferns.

Ferns are primitive plants, reproducing by spores which usually appear on the underside of the frond in clusters called *sori*. They go through an amazing life cycle before a new plant like the parent is produced. They are fascinating to grow—some are very easy—some are very difficult.

Before you buy a fern . . .

Ask yourself these questions:

What sort of fern do I want—big, little, house, hanging, intricate?

What demands does the fern have?—light, humidity, watering?

Can I furnish that kind of place and care?

Will it have to adjust from being in a greenhouse to my place? What can I do to make the transition to different conditions possible?

How soon will it need repotting?

Answer these questions, find the right fern, and with consistent care, you can have marvelous results with ferns, but—
—BEWARE, you can become addicted to ferns!

Here are some of the easiest to grow: Your first ones might be plants with leathery fronds; there are many that have very intricately divided fronds, and they're hardy.

Rabbit's Foot	*Davallia fejeensis*
Squirrel's Foot	*Davallia trichomanoides*
Leather Fern	*Rumohra adiantiformis*
House Holly	*Cyrtomium falcatum*
Button Fern	*Pellaea rotundifolia*

When these thrive, try these next:

Mother Fern	*Asplenium bulbiferum*
Bird's Nest	*Asplenium nidus*
Boston Fern	*Nephrolepis exaltata* var *Bostoniensis* and its cultivars
Rosy Maidenhair	*Adiantum hispidulum*
Five Finger	*Adiantum pedatum*
	Pteris cretica cv Ouvrardii (this is hardy outside the easiest of all *Pteris*)
Hare's Foot	*Polypodium aureum*

And then on to some hardy, outside ones:

Christmas Fern	*Polystichum acrostichoides*
Western Sword	*Polystichum munitum*
Lady Fern	*Athyrium filix-femina*
Soft Shield	*Polystichum setiferum* and its cultivars

Growing Mixes

There are many different mixes that can be used for ferns. Essentially they should be as similar to the natural soils the ferns grow in as possible. The most important ingredient is richness of organic matter—humus, peat moss, compost, bark, or shavings—which not only provides a base for the fern to grow in but also much of the necessary nutrients. Moreover, it helps retain moisture, for ferns like to grow in damp situations; however, most ferns must also have good drainage. Therefore sand is added to the organic materials to allow the water to drain out slowly, thus preventing "sog." There are notable exceptions to this, for there are water-loving ferns which grow naturally in marshes or swamps such as the Royal Osmunda *(Osmunda regalis)* and some varieties of the Spinulose Wood Fern *(Dryopteris spinulosa)*.

So, your mix must contain both humus material and sand. Whichever of the following mixes you use, moisten it at least a few hours before you plant your fern—planting in moist mix will help minimize transplant "shock."

Commercial mixes like Black Gold, African Violet Mix, and House Plant Potting Mix are all somewhat acceptable, but usually do not contain enough humus nor enough material to make it sufficiently porous, so add one part peat moss and one part sand to two parts commercial mix. Then add two tablespoons of bonemeal to each two gallons. You may discover that these organic mixes also contain perlite (a white, inorganic material which helps to provide soil aeration), vermiculite (a shiny, flaky substance that gives it lightness), and often bits of charcoal (especially useful in terrariums.) You may want to add even more of these substances. Remember, ferns need mix which is one-half to three-fourths organic material. Many houseplant mixes are too heavy and solid.

If you want to make your own mixes, here are some recipes:

Simple mix

  1 part peat moss
  1 part sharp sand

Garden loam mix

  3 part peat moss
  1 part garden loam (no clay)
  1 part sand

To each gallon above, add
  2 tablespoons bone meal

Rich fern mix

  2 parts peat moss
  1 part fine fir bark
  1 part sharp sand

To each gallon above, add
  2 tablespoons of bone meal

You may want to sift these (or even the commercial mixes) through a piece of screening to make them fine in texture for young or small ferns. Be sure the sand is not from an ocean beach with its saltiness.

For ferns, like basket ferns held in place by sphagnum moss, or ones which need especially good drainage, add to the recipe of your choice:

1 part coarse bark
1 part vermiculite or perlite

Plants in coarse mix will need water more frequently than those in fine mixes.

For lime-loving (alkaline soil) ferns

2 parts peat moss
2 parts vermiculite
1 part sharp sand

For each 2 gallons, add 5 tablespoons oyster shell and 2 tablespoons bone meal.

For plants in your garden, be sure the soil is rich in organic matter (leaves, compost). If it isn't, add enough peat moss so the soil is at least half organic. Be sure to add much coarse sand and bark if your soil is clayey or if the soil tends to pack. Ferns must have drainage. Or, you can dig out the original soil in the spots for ferns, replacing it with one of the mixes. If your soil is too sandy, add peat moss and/or bark to reach the one-half organic rule. Dig the bed deeply, and since organic matter slowly breaks down, it must be replaced after two or three years. Sprinkling peat moss or other organic materials on the surface helps reduce moisture loss, but these materials should also be dug in around your ferns as the original materials decompose and are used up.

Watering

Most house ferns need water at least twice a week, depending on the temperature and humidity in the room. Top watering is probably best—pour water into the pot until it begins to drain into the saucer. Check the saucer in a half hour and pour off any additional water that has drained through—don't let ferns stand in water.

Big pots are probably best watered by setting them in a sink or tub and letting them soak up from the bottom till the top begins to show it is moist. Two or three times a week may be enough watering. Most ferns demand good drainage and should never be overwatered. If the pot is in a decorative outer pot that has no drain hole, check regularly to see if water has accumulated there; if so, pour it off.

Use rain water whenever possible and if you live in an area of hard water, use distilled water. Leaching—pouring water into the pot until it runs out the bottom freely—is excellent for all houseplants at least every two months.

If your plant calls for moist soil conditions, water when the soil surface is still slightly damp, but don't keep it soggy. If plant calls for moist/dry conditions (as Leather Fern, *Rumohra adiantiformis*), don't water until the soil surface is slightly dry, but not dried out. Some ferns specifically shouldn't be watered until they are dry—those ferns especially can't stand too much water.

If your ferns call for humid conditions, you can use a tray of pebbles to set the pots on. Have it 2.5-3 cm (1'') deep with small pebbles, then add water till it is 1 cm deep. Do not let the water level rise to root level—this rots the roots. Evaporation from the tray will definitely raise the humidity around the fern plants. Also it will help if you group the plants that need humidity together. Of course, misting them is also very helpful.

For outside ferns, test down below the surface to see when they need water. Deep, occasional watering is much better than frequent shallow watering, for it gets the soil evenly moist, doesn't drive the oxygen out of the soil, and helps wash out alkali that accumulates with many types of hard water. Excessive watering promotes bacterial growth, and the roots of the ferns may rot and soil becomes sour. Mulch the area with redwood sawdust or leaf mold to retain moisture.

Fertilizing

A good rich planting mix used for growing your ferns naturally provides the nutrients the plant needs, so a newly transplanted fern does not need to be (and should not be) fertilized. However, after two weeks to two months, a simple schedule of regular fertilizing will help keep your fern green, growing and gorgeous. If you want to have it grow slowly, however, and remain small, give it half the schedule or half the strength that is suggested for that fern. The color of the fronds gives you a clue as to whether the fern needs fertilizer.

Fertilizers should be "low burn" for best results—meaning those that have a low percentage of salts which dissolve easily in water. Liquid fertilizers are far safer for your ferns than dry fertilizers, for you can control their concentration. Dry fertilizers may last longer, but the uniform distribution of even the powder forms is a problem. There are both organic (originally from living material) and inorganic (from chemical or mining processes) liquid fertilizers. Fish emulsion and bone meal are organic while chemicals like superphosphate and ammonium sulfate are inorganic. Examples of liquid organic fertilizers with low burn characteristics are fish emulsion, Spoonit, Blue Whale, Hyponex, and Schulz Instant liquid plant food.

In the descriptions of individual ferns, beginning on page 31, it is usually suggested that you use half or a quarter of the strength or concentration recommended by the manufacturer of the fertilizer. Measure and mix carefully; be a reliable mixer for your ferns. This will help you decide if what you're giving is too much or too little after you have had it awhile and get acquainted with it. Generally speaking, one-fourth strength every two weeks is a good basic schedule. As some say: "weakly, weekly." Mark your calendar, and do it regularly; do the regular watering, then fertilize. If you don't want a fern to grow too fast, don't feed it quite as often, but *don't* feed it twice as much to make it grow fast—this may do it in.

Knowing when not to fertilize is important too: Don't fertilize newly transplanted ferns—hold off for at least two weeks. Don't fertilize when your plant seems to be entering a "rest period." This is more true of outside ferns than house ferns. Wait till you see signs of new croziers, then resume your regular schedule. Don't fertilize if your fern shows, by burned fronds or sudden wilting of fronds, that something is wrong. Instead, pour a lot of water on the soil, let it drain thoroughly, then water lightly for awhile.

Light

All ferns need at least some light; most require filtered or indirect light. Dim, dark rooms will need artificial light for ferns to do well. Outside ferns vary from being able to take considerable sun to no sun. The light requirements for each fern are given in the individual write-ups.

In general, *low light* means shade outside, near a north window or back from an east window inside. However, if you live in the north, the amount of light from those windows is not adequate, so you'll need to move your fern near an east window or use artificial light. In southern areas, next to a north window might prove to be too light, especially if the light is reflected off the neighbor's white wall. Study your situation, and move your plant to find the optimum spot.

Medium light means semishade, diffused or indirect light—no sun, unless it is through leaves, a thin curtain, or other filter. It can be at most any window depending on the curtains or bushes, trees, walls, etc., outside.

High light means bright reflected light or some sun. It is best to have this sunlight in early morning or later afternoon, for midday sun is just too hot and intense for most ferns.

Even ferns not wanting high light situations may take some early morning sun and flourish, especially in the winter.

North and east situations, either outside or inside, are generally best for ferns. Exposed southern and western sites usually are far too hot and bright. These areas, of course, can be excellent sites for ferns if they are modified by trees, shrubs, curtains, roof overhang, lattice, plastic or cloth shelters, and sufficient humidity.

Fluorescent lights used for a few to many hours daily are often a solution for indoor plants. A regular electric light gives off too much heat. Cool white, using one or two tubes, is a good choice. Effect is very minimal further than 30 cm (12") sidewards or 60 cm (24") below. Reflectors or aluminum foil beneath the ferns will increase the intensity.

As fall approaches, you may have to move houseplants nearer windows or to other light source. Move them before they get leggy and pale. Be careful of bright winter sun close to windows, especially midday. As spring comes, remember to move them further away again. Outdoors be sure that deciduous trees which gave partial shade to your ferns still give enough shade from the less intense winter sun. And if there is unusual weather producing a series of brilliantly sunny, warm days, you may have to shade them temporarily.

Suggestions: Because room colors, shapes, trees outside, light colored walls, walks, etc. all affect the light conditions, you may have to keep moving your ferns until you find where they're happy in your particular situation.

Grooming

All ferns look best if regularly groomed. When and how this is done depends on whether they are indoor or outdoor plants, and the season of the year. Always use sharp scissors or small, narrow-tipped pruners.

During the growing season, for both house and outdoor ferns, cut off the whole frond near soil surface if it looks injured, dead, or is doing poorly. If only the tip is bruised and

turns brown, the frond can be cut just back of the brown
area. You can even reshape the frond by careful trimming.
Also a damaged pinna or two can be snipped off, making the
whole plant look better.

At the end of the growing season outdoors, it is often best
to just let the old fronds be, to protect the fern crown during
the winter. The colder and snowier the area you live in, the
more important this protection becomes. In the spring, the
old fronds and accumulated leaves can be carefully removed.
Never rake leaves off fern areas—the croziers form early, are
tender and are easily broken. It is best to crumble any dry
leaves and fronds by hand and let them settle back on the
crowns to provide late frost protection and humus for
nutrients.

Houseplants generally do not go through a dormant
period, though they may slow down. Be sure they don't get
too hot by being too near windows when the sun is at a low
angle or in the way of forced air outlets. Also watch for spots
that may have drafts when outside doors are opened—ferns
do not thrive on quick temperature and humidity changes.
Grouping ferns together or using pebble trays will help keep
the humidity more even.

Propagation,
or how to get more ferns

There are many ways to increase your fern collection:

Above Ground Rhizomes
Many ferns can be divided by cutting pieces of the rhizomes.
This is especially true of ferns like the Rabbit's Foot and
Squirrel's Foot types *(Davallias,* etc.) which produce creeping, above-ground rhizomes from which the new fronds
grow. Simply take a sharp knife and cut off outreaching
rhizomes back from the growing tip far enough so there are
roots on those portions. You can take pieces that don't have
roots but those will grow much more slowly. Carefully

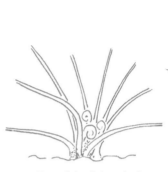

Creeping rhizome, fronds
spaced 8 + cm apart

Fronds in tight spiral

Forming dense clumps

Tree fern

Creeping rhizome, fronds
closely spaced, 1 ± cm

remove them from the basket or soil surface, disturbing the roots as little as possible. Fill a container with mix to within an inch of the top, pressing it down gently. Use commercial mix with additional sand and peat moss or a mix of one part peat moss and one part sand or vermiculite. Do not use soil or compost in these mixes for they are more apt to contain fungus spores. Gently insert the cut end diagonally into the mix, burying the roots, but do not cover the rhizomes. Hold the rhizome piece in place, if necessary, with small hairpins. Keep shady and moist (misting helps), but don't overwater.

Division of Underground Rhizomes
Ferns which spread with underground rhizomes can also be divided in a similar fashion. Decide where they can be separated; then cut down through with a sharp knife. Be sure you separate a piece with enough root system to support the fronds. If it is a garden fern, you can either dig up the whole clump and then divide it or leave it in the ground and use a sharp shovel to make the cut, and then lift out one portion. Be sure to fill in the hole with proper and sufficient fern mix. Always be careful to disturb the roots as little as possible. You will probably want to cut off some of the older fronds to give the transplant a chance to get situated. This is also a good time to groom the plants. Keep them moist and in less light than usual for a few days. Fertilize with one-fourth strength liquid organic fertilizer in two weeks.

Divisions of Clumps
Clump ferns, as Maidenhairs, Boston Ferns, etc., can be divided easily. Usually late in the winter or early spring is the best time. If the pot is too crowded, gently tap out the whole plant (hold the leaves carefully in one hand, turn the pot upside down and tap edge on working surface). Lay the clump on its side and carefully separate the fronds into two groups—you may have to untangle interlacing fronds. Then try to do likewise with the fibrous roots, without knocking off any more soil than is necessary. With a clean, sharp knife, cut through the fibrous root mass and gently pull the

two sections apart. Repot with good fern mix, appropriate to the kind of fern, and gently push the soil down around the roots; water immediately. Keep the new plant in a shadier, more humid place for a few days. If the clumps are in the ground, follow suggestions for Division of Underground Rhizomes. Always remember to water thoroughly but gently.

Fernlets
Several ferns will produce baby plants right on their fronds. Mother Fern *(Asplenium bulbiferum)* is one of the best-known, with tiny fernlets developing on the upper surfaces of the bigger fronds. The Hand Fern *(Doryopteris pedata* var *palmata)* develops plantlets at the base of both sterile and fertile fronds. The Soft Shield Fern, *Polystichum setiferum* and its cultivars produce dozens of buds along the rachis. Some of the *Woodwardias* also produce frond buds. These buds can develop into new plants and there are several methods to grow them.

The fastest method is to leave the frond on the parent plant, bending the frond down to a nearby planting surface (use commercial mix with added sand and vermiculite or one part peat moss, one part sand, and one part vermiculite). Predampen this mix and hold the frond down on the mix with small wire hairpins. The frond keeps supplying water and food to the developing fernlets until they are big enough to carry on alone. Be sure the planting surface is kept moist, but don't overwater.

You may also cut off the whole frond or pieces with buds, fastening them to the predampened mix with hairpins or sand. Then it is best to cover with Saran Wrap or glass for awhile to keep the humidity high, but watch that they do not become overly damp, for mold can be a menace. Peek occasionally to see how they are doing—this will also help to keep them from becoming too moist. Gradually remove the covering as the fernlets begin to take hold and at that time snip off old frond bits.

The little fernlets may also be removed from the fronds

when they have two or three little leaves 1-2 cm long. Usually
they can be pricked off. Carefully place them about an inch
apart on the premoistened mix for rooting, gently push the
mix around them at the base. Cover the pot with Saran or
glass to keep the humidity high. Raise the cover occasionally
to prevent too much moisture accumulating (you will want to
see how they are doing anyway). When the fernlets have
grown roots and bigger leaves (3-4 cm long), carefully move
them so each can have more room. This is the crucial time
for they can dry out quickly. Keep them moist, but don't let
them sog. Enclosing the pot in a plastic bag with a hole is a
good plan—enlarging the hole gradually as the fernlets grow,
until finally the bag can be removed. Too much humidity can
make the fern turn brown and/or mold.

Staghorn Pups

Staghorn Ferns produce "pups" from the roots of the
parent, showing first as buds on the shield frond, eventually
producing their own little shields and arching fronds. These
pups can be cut off carefully when they have several little
shield fronds of their own. This is best done in the spring.
Cut behind the pup's oldest shield, and if you get a bit of the
mother's shield, so much the better. Plant the pups in an
upright position on a pad of spaghnum moss fastened to a
piece of bark or board or in the side of a broken pot lined
with moss and filled with coarse peat. Tie the pup to the pot
with plastic tape or noncopper wire. Water it well and then
hang it up to drip. Mist regularly but not heavily for a couple
of weeks, then water as for Staghorns.

Stalk Propagation

Hart's Tongue Fern can produce new plants from the base of
the fleshy stalks. Remove a whole frond, cutting it at the
base of the stalk. Insert it into damp rooting mix (one part
fine peat moss, one part sand, one part vermiculite) and keep
the mix damp but not wet.

Runners

Boston Ferns and their exotic cultivars produce long, scaly runners. These will easily root at their tip in the garden, and even those in pots may develop little plantlets with fronds and tiny roots right there in the moist air. You can let these runners rest in a nearby pot, and when sufficiently big and rooted, snip the connecting runner and have a new fern.

Crown Ferns

Ferns which grow from a definite crown which does not produce root buds of any kind cannot be divided. New plants must be raised from spores.

Growing Ferns from Spores

This is a fun way to increase your ferns—or to get new ones from other people or native ferns without removing those plants. However, it does take some time and effort. Spore growing is, of course, the usual way ferns reproduce—a method that is fairly easy to follow and certainly fascinating to watch, as the fern goes through its amazing cycle before another plant appears of the type we think of as a fern.

First: Collect spores. Examine the underside of the fronds, using at least a 10x magnifier. The spores are produced in clusters of sporangia called sori, in different arrangements and patterns on different ferns. Each sori is usually covered by a thin membrane called an *indusium*. If this indusium is green, the spores are too young. Gradually the color will change, becoming tan, brown, blackish, or even reddish. The sori should look fat and unopened. If the sori are flat or cracked or ragged, the spore cases have already opened and the spores are gone. When you find fat sori, cut off the frond, or part of it and place it, sori side down on a piece of clean, smooth paper in an out-of-the-way, dry, non-breezy area. Or put the fronds in an envelope, and let the spores drop off into that sealed area. Within three to seven days, the spores should have dropped. Sometimes they are so abundant they reproduce the frond pattern. There usually is a fair amount of debris with them—the spores are very tiny and look like very fine powder, not grainy. Carefully tip the paper or envelope and shake those bigger pieces off. Now fold the paper up around the spores in a neat package, label, and date. Usually the sooner spores are planted after being collected the better.

Second: Prepare pots and mix. Thoroughly scrub with hot water as many clay pots and saucers as you have different kinds of spores. (Some people prefer well-scrubbed plastic or foam pots. In that case, omit step three). Dip the pots into 10% clorox solution (1 part clorox to 9 parts water), and rinse them in hot water. These procedures not only clean the pots but also thoroughly prewet them. Make one of the following mixes:

#1 3 parts fine peat moss
    1 part sharp sand

#2 2 parts sifted garden loam
    2 parts fine peat moss
    1 part sharp sand

Put the mixes through a fine screen (window screen), and then thoroughly wet them. If you are sporing *Adiantums* or other ferns needing lime, add a bit of fine oyster shell.

Fill the pot to within 3-4 cm (1.5'') of the top with mix, gently leveling the surface.

Third: Sterilize pots and soil. Fill the saucers at least half full of water, set pots in them and place both sections in 250° oven for two hours. Remove and lay a clean piece of paper over each until they thoroughly cool (another couple of hours).

Fourth: Taking one pot at a time, remove the cover paper, unfold a spore packet and by carefully tapping the paper, sprinkle the spores evenly over the soil surface. Cover with Saran Wrap held tightly in place with a rubber band. Add the date of planting to the label, and slip it under the rubber band. Place the pots in warm area (65-80°), but not in direct sun (under fluorescent lights is excellent). Again fill the saucer half full with boiled water (if it has all been evaporated by oven treatment), and bide your time. Whenever all the water from the saucer has been used, again fill them half full.

After a few days, or many, many days depending on the kinds of ferns, a tinge of green will appear. These are the tiny prothallia—the tiny, heart-shaped plants which grow from fern spores. In time they each may reach 1 cm (1/3'') or so in diameter, and look much like liverworts—not at all like the fern plant that produced the spores. The prothallia produce female and male cells, which unite under moist conditions, and from those fertilized cells the new sporophyte fern plants grow. Most people want to peek every few days or so—go ahead— it's fun to see the green tinge get greener and finally become little prothallia, but don't peek for long and do cover again tightly.

When these prothallia have definite form, though still very tiny, they should be carefully pricked out and replanted. Fill a well scrubbed flat with one of the premoistened mixes given above. Gently press the surface with a board (so no big air spaces are left), then lift out little groups of the prothallia about the size of half a thumbnail and place in a small dent you've made in the planting mix. The upper end of a pair of tweezers is a good instrument—do not handle any more than is necessary and be very gentle. Press the mix around the group, and continue, planting these little groups about 2 cm apart. When the flat is filled, mist it well with distilled water, and cover with Saran Wrap or glass. Actually a little frame with heavier plastic is better, for it gives head room to the little sporophytes that will soon be growing. Keep the flat in a warm, lighted, but not sunny location. Mist it regularly, for moisture is an absolute necessity for the movement of the male cells.

The prothallia will grow, and when little ferns with upright leaves begin to appear these clumps should be divided again. Prick them out using a sharp knife, pointed wooden or plastic implement, and transplant them into prepared flats, again leaving 2-3 cm between each. A mix of 3 parts fine peat moss, 1 part sharp sand and 1 part vermiculite is good. Moisten it well, then load up the flat, leveling and gently pressing with a board. Parts of the prothallia may still be present, but will gradually disappear as the new ferns develop. The roots are often amazingly long. Mist the transplants well, keep in a moist, shady place and water whenever necessary, but don't overwater. This is a very crucial time, and going dry once will finish them off. In two weeks, you can start a regular, every two week schedule of fertilizing with one-fourth strength liquid organic fertilizer. When plants are big enough, move them into separate pots and treat as for that species.

Transpotting

Many ferns appear to thrive when their roots are crowded (Boston Fern is one of these), but the time eventually comes when the fern is too big for its container.

Depending on your desires and the kind of fern, you can divide it and plant each piece in a pot the size the original plant was in, or you can repot it in a bigger container. In these plants the root mass is usually very solid—the plant is rootbound and the fibrous roots more or less fill the pot with no room for soil. So, choose a considerably bigger pot, but before replanting, take a stick, your fingers, a large crochet hook or some such tool and break that mass apart somewhat. Generally you'll find that the roots tend to hang together on the outer edge, leaving an open space in the middle. So—place your potting soil in the new pot so it is heaped up in the middle, fit the roots down around it and then add more mix. Gently push the soil down, especially around the edge so it is in contact with the roots and will also hold the plant in position. Be sure to leave enough space at the top of the pot for watering.

Problems with Ferns: Growing Conditions and Pests

The best way to prevent problems with your ferns is to keep them healthy in the first place. Give each fern the conditions it thrives in, watering, feeding, grooming it regularly. Be sure they have adequate light, that the soil conditions are right, and that they are in the proper mix and drain well enough. Some environmental problems which might develop and their symptoms are listed below:

Long and spindly, few fronds, thin, yellowish	too little light
Small, yellowish, thicker-than-usual fronds, poor growth.	too much light
Fronds thinnish, brownish spots on smooth fronds, Boston ferns shed foliage; fungus diseases invade	too much humidity
Poor growth, lower leaves yellowish, stems soft, soil soggy	too much water
Fronds, especially the edges, curled and brown, poor growth, leaves light green. . . .	too little water
Young growth often shriveled, edges brown.	too little humidity, or in draft, windy spot, or too cold
New leaves small and slow to grow	too little fertilizer
New growth rapid but weak, white crust builds up on soil and on edge of pot	too much fertilizer
Fronds or parts of fronds burned and dry	too hot or too much light

| Leaves suddenly turn yellow and droop . . . . | too sudden a temperature change |
| Plant perks up, then droops after watering . . . . | probably too crowded |

Watch for insects or small animals before they become abundant. Puckering of the leaves, curling under of the edges, pieces gone from the frond, or white flies flying out when foliage is disturbed are signs that something is wrong. As you care for your ferns, watch for trouble signs.

Fern aphids are tiny, blackish sucking insects especially found on young, tender areas. They secrete a sticky "honeydew" which may be your first recognition of them, and a black mold may develop in those areas. Ants feed on this honeydew and actually "herd" aphids around. Keep the ants under control and aphids and mealy bugs will not be such a problem. If you catch them soon enough, spray with warm soapy water (½ teaspoon mild detergent to 1 gallon water) for either outdoors or house plants, or dunk them in the warm soapy water, always rinse with clear tepid water. Repeat a time or two if necessary. Some people find that aphids on houseplants or outdoor pots can be controlled by putting a no-pest insect strip in a plastic bag, pulling the bag over the plant, closing it as much as possible, leaving the bag on for only one-half hour. Wash hands after handling strip. If that doesn't do the job, you may have to use a chemical spray. However, many ferns, especially the Maidenhairs, Boston Ferns, *Pteris,* and *Aspleniums* are damaged with chemical sprays so try to control with other methods. If you must use chemical sprays, do it outdoors and cut the concentration at least in half. Malathion is a foliage spray, meta-systox-R and Cygon are systemic, and can be used to drench the soil, thus cutting down foliage burn. It usually takes about three weeks for results. Mix only the amount needed and keep sprays well-labeled and away from children and pets.

Mealy bugs are tiny sucking insects covered with a whitish powder or wax. If there aren't too many, dab them with a cotton swab dipped in rubbing alcohol; then wash your fern with warm soapy water (½ teaspoon to gallon of water), and rinse in clear tepid water. If you need to use a chemical spray, do it outside as for aphids. Reduce the concentration by one-half or one-fourth.

Scales are sucking insects which are seen as small, shiny, elongated bumps, especially on the veins on the under side. If there aren't many, use a cotton swab dipped in corn oil or warm soapy water (see aphids). First scrub them gently with a toothbrush, then spray. Rinse with clear water. If more drastic treatment is required, treat as for aphids. Sword Ferns and Button Ferns seem particularly to be their favorites.

Snails and slugs may be pests, especially on tender plants. Watch for their slimy tracks and make a ring of bait around the plant before they've eaten too much. Put well away from center of fern, for some baits mold. Silver Brake *(Pteris argyrea)* and Maidenhairs are favorites.

Spider mites, also called Red Spider Mites, do not seem to bother true ferns particularly, but the Asparagus Ferns are susceptible. They are almost microscopic—(use handlens) but are detected by fine white webs on the underside and pale or whitish specks or areas develop on the foliage. Spider Mites are healthiest when the humidity is low—so if you get them, increase the humidity, and then spray with Pentac (take plants outside).

White flies may bother your ferns if you have other plants infected with them. Spray outside, using malathion if the soapy solution (see aphids) doesn't work. Use one-half the normal concentration of the spray. Note also the ferns that can't take chemical sprays on their foliage (see aphids).

Fungus may be a problem when growing spores. Be sure to sterilize pots and soil (see spore growing) and disinfect trays used for transplanting prothallia or sporelings. To disinfect, use 1½ teaspoon Dexon and ½ teaspoon Terrachlor per gallon of water.

Ferns

Tender—nights not below 60°F. . . . . T
Semi-Tender—nights not below 50°F. . . . . ST

An E in the margin means easy-to-grow. The name of each
fern illustrated is followed by a percentage indicating its size
compared to the actual size. For example, an illustration
labeled 45% is less than half the size of a typical frond from
that fern.

Special Maidenhairs

There are many, many cultivars of Maidenhairs available in
florist shops, and at times even in local supermarkets. Most
of these are fairly temperamental to raise since they have just
come from a greenhouse and therefore go into shock easily
when put in your less-than-humid house. It's best to be successful with less temperamental ones, such as Southern Maidenhair (*Adiantum raddianum* (49)) and Rosy Maidenhair
(*Adiantum hispidulum* (50)), then tackle these.

Adiantum raddianum cv Pacific Maid is probably one of the   **ST**
easiest of the fluffy Maidenhair cultivars to grow, for its
temperature demands are less. It needs low to medium light
and high humidity. Bathrooms or kitchens are probably the
best spots in the house, particularly if you use pebble trays. It
is disappointing and tragic to see a lovely Maidenhair turn
brown and die, but then, you may have just the place and
touch for them.

Adiantum tenerum cv Farleyense is an airy, ruffly Maiden-   **T**
hair. It is difficult to grow and does best in greenhouses
where the temperature and humidity are kept higher than in
homes.

Adiantum capillus-veneris cv Imbricatus, called Green Pet-   **ST**
ticoat is a ruffly one with large, overlapping fan-shaped
leaflets. It is easier than *A. tenerum* cv Farleyense to grow,
but generally it needs greenhouse conditions or a specially
humid, constant temperature spot.

31

ST *Adiantum raddianum* cv Triumph is a cultivar with many, tiny, tear-shaped, heart-shaped, or mitten-shaped pinnules, giving the plant a filmy, airy appearance. It needs low to medium light, high humidity (greenhouse, bathroom, or moist shady spot in the garden, especially if hanging). Be sure it has good drainage. Once it gets established, it will do well as a special indoor plant.

Fertilize all these cultivars every two or three weeks with one-fourth strength organic liquid fertilizer during the growing season. Keep them well groomed. Be sure they have some lime in their soil, that they have adequate moisture, but that they drain well.

PACIFIC MAID (80%)

IMBRICATUS (45%)

TRIUMPH (35%)

33

Dwarf Mother Fern; Mauritius Spleenwort
Asplenium daucifolium (viviparum)

ST   The Dwarf Mother Fern is a neat little fern with narrow pinnae and slender, almost thread-like pinnules. It is more
tender than the regular Mother Fern and needs a more humid
spot, so it is an excellent dwarf for terrariums. It can be
grown in pots in the house by using pebble trays, grouping
ferns, or by misting often. However, if it is too humid, the
fronds will turn brownish. Water frequently enough to keep
the soil uniformly moist, but not wet.

It is truly a dwarf, and usually doesn't grow larger than 25
cm (10''). Like Mother Fern, this also produces buds on the
fronds which develop into tiny new ferns. These little fernlets
have tiny first leaves that are much different from the parent.
These fernlets easily reproduce the plant (see propagation).

Dwarf Mother Fern likes low light—a north window is
fine—and wants high humidity and night temperature above
50°F. Always keep the soil moist, but the amount of water
they need during the winter is far less than during its more
active growing time. This will depend on conditions in your
home, but watch that you don't overwater; particularly be
sure that if the pot is in a pebble tray that the bottom of the
pot doesn't reach the water.

Fertilize every two weeks with one-fourth strength organic
liquid fertilizer during late spring to late fall, but cut to once
a month during winter. Repot in late winter if needed.

DWARF MOTHER FERN (30%)

Bird's Nest Fern
Asplenium nidus

Bird's Nest Fern is a shiny, apple-green, beautiful fern with undivided, broad fronds and prominent black midribs. Each wavy-edged frond has a slender, narrow base, changing quite rapidly to a broader upper portion which then tapers rapidly at the tip. **E**
ST

The common name, Bird's Nest, was given because of the hairy, fuzzy central crown, the fronds growing from the outer rim of this crown. This is one of the easy ferns to grow, for it needs less humidity than many ferns. Never let water stand in the "bird's nest," for that may cause rot. The fronds usually grow to be 30-40 cm (12-16") long, but may become much longer in lush conditions. Lovely as the fronds are, resist the temptation to touch them for they bruise fairly easily.

It is an excellent house plant, flourishing in fairly small pots. It prefers nighttime temperature not below 50° or 60 °F and daytime temperature not below 70°F. Brown spots may appear on the fronds if it gets too cold or too wet. It does well outside on a shady patio in the summer. Turn it occasionally so it keeps its symmetry. It likes high to medium light, and even filtered sunlight.

BIRD'S NEST (20%)

Pot with rich soil mix. Water enough so soil is moist, but not excessively, cutting down on the amount in the winter months. Fertilize once a month with one-fourth strength liquid organic fertilizer.

This fern can be raised from spores, but sori are produced only on large, mature fronds; houseplants seldom produce them. If you want more Bird's Nests, best to watch for young ones, then buy and repot in late winter. They prefer fairly shallow pots. Don't fertilize for the first month.

Rabbit's Foot; Fiji Davallia
Davallia fejeensis

E
ST
This small-to-medium sized fern resembles Squirrel's Foot *(Davallia trichomanoides),* but is even more finely divided and lacy. The fronds are larger and the hairy rhizomes tend to be browner or more reddish. It is not as hardy, however, but will do well outside on sheltered patios in temperate areas.

This fern grows especially well in hanging baskets. Be sure it has enough potting mix with added humus to hold moisture but enough sand or perlite to provide good drainage. It also looks very natural if planted on a thick piece of bark or fern trunk or hollow porous lava rock. If planted so, watch its watering needs. Probably it is best to set the bark on a tray with pebbles which you can keep damp.

Although it grows well outside in temperate areas, it does enjoy winter heat, so you may want to bring it into a slightly warmer area such as a hallway. However, be careful of drafts.

Grows easily from rhizome cutting (see propagation). Use one-fourth strength liquid organic fertilizer every two weeks during active growing season.

It is a native of Australia.

RABBIT'S FOOT (50%)

Hand Fern
Doryopteris pedata var *palmata*

T   This small tender fern has very unusual, beautiful bright
green fronds. The first fronds, and the sterile fronds, are
smaller and resemble maple leaves. The fertile fronds are on
taller stalks with slender pointed segments between the deep
lobes—almost a snowflake pattern. The sori are in a continuous narrow band around the edge of each.

Hand Fern is an excellent house fern, especially in a large
terrarium, for it wants high humidity, night temperature no
lower than 60°F and only medium light, with no direct sun.
It should be kept on the moist side, but be sure your planting
mix drains well.

The fronds arise in a tuft from a short rhizome; the
croziers are covered with tightly packed scales. The stalk at
first is greenish with scattered tan scales near base but turns
brownish as it develops, and the mature frond has a wiry,
chocolate-brown stalk. The clump spreads slowly from root
buds. Fertilize every three months at one-half strength.

An unusual feature of this plant is that new fernlets
develop at the base of both fertile and sterile fronds just at
the top of the stalk. These may be plucked off, planted in
rich potting mix.

HAND FERN (30%)

Boston Fern
Nephrolepis exaltata var *Bostoniensis*

This natural variation was first discovered near Boston in the late 1800s. It had wider and more graceful fronds than the usual form, and the many cultivars now available have been developed from it.

E
T

It is an easy houseplant to grow (or outside in mild climates) especially in hanging pots so the fronds can show to best advantage. It can take varied light conditions, from low to high light, but no direct sun. Find under which conditions it flourishes for you by moving it occasionally. Does well with fluorescent light, as in many offices. The fronds will become a pale green if they do not have enough light. Also be sure they have good air circulation but not cold drafts, for that dramatically changes the temperature. They prefer to be no colder than 50 °F at night and 68 °-72 °F during the day.

Use good humus soil with extra peat and sand, or potting mix with extra sand. They like to be evenly moist, but must not be soggy. The soil should be just barely moist before rewatering. People tend to overwater this fern.

Potted plants do well if transplanted into humus garden soils in shady, moist areas in the summer, or hang the pots in

BOSTON FERN (20%)

shady areas. They will take more water in the summer than in the winter, but again, don't overwater.

Boston Ferns are generally sterile plants, not producing spores, but established plants grow long, thin, scaly runners. These will eventually produce a new plant at the tip, with tiny roots and fronds if the air is moist enough or if you are using a basket, pin them to the edge of the moss. Cut these off (midsummer is probably the best time) and pot in good fern mix. These grow into good-sized plants fairly rapidly. Grow new plants and occasionally replace the old ones when they seem to get tired.

If you keep to a fertilizing schedule, the fern may soon be fairly crowded if the pot was small. They like a little room around the side of the pot. When the fronds crowd the edge, repot or divide. The old fronds tend to die back at that time. As soon as the new fronds appear, cut the old ones off.

Boston Fern Cultivars

There are dozens of exotic cultivars now available, with fantastically varied fronds that are ruffled or frilled or intricately divided. They tend to have a more compact form than their long-legged ancestor, and generally do not grow as rapidly, nor are they quite as easy to grow. However, they can be grown very well as lovely houseplants, especially if you remember that they prefer moist/dry conditions, meaning they like plenty of water but don't need rewatering till the soil feels almost dry. Generally speaking, the finer the foliage the less water is needed (and people often overwater, thinking that plants with fine and delicate foliage need much water). If the air is very dry in the house, misting will help, though grouping ferns seems to be more effective.

Be sure the soil mix has plenty of humus, and sand, for they must drain well. Fertilize regularly, every two weeks with one-fourth strength liquid organic fertilizer, except when the plant is not actively growing. Many nurseries fertilize with very weak solutions almost every time they water—thus the saying "weekly, weakly."

They vary in their light demands and can take low to high light—move them occasionally to see which they like best in your situation and also turn them every so often. They can be cool at night (to 50 °F), but they prefer daytime temperatures of 68 °-72 °F.

These ferns with their frilly, frothy foliage may often have inside fronds or individual pinnae turn brown. This may happen even to healthy ferns. Cut the frond or pinna off, and this will allow more light to get to younger fronds (but check to be sure you aren't overwatering). If you object to the thin, scaly runners which develop, just cut them off.

Probably your fern, even if given the best of care, won't be perfect all the time—groom Boston Ferns heavily when they need it, reducing water for awhile and display another fern in that spot, giving your Boston cultivar a rest period.

Some Boston Fern Cultivars

Nephrolepis exaltata cv compacta: a dwarf Boston Fern with   T
fairly upright fronds only to 45 cm (18'')—a very successful and easy houseplant.

Nephrolepis exaltata cv Florida Ruffle: A lovely cultivar   T
with quite dense fronds; each pinna is wider and regularly, but deeply, cut from about midway to the tip, giving the frond an ruffly-edge appearance.

Nephrolepis exaltata cv Fluffy Ruffles is very similar to   T
Florida Ruffles but never grows fronds longer than about 30 cm (12'').

Nephrolepis exaltata cv Trevillian: A truly beautiful cultivar   T
with the pinnules deeply cut or divided towards the tip of each, producing beautiful 3-dimentional, lacy fronds. The fronds arch and drape gracefully, and may be 60 cm (2') long and 20 cm (8'') wide.

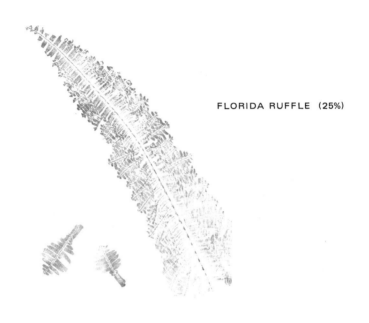

FLORIDA RUFFLE (25%)

TREVILLIAN (25%)

42

Maidenhair Cliff Brake
Pellaea viridis var *macrophyla (P. adiantoides)*

The fronds of this fern are somewhat similar to a Maidenhair **ST** in shape and veinage; also it has shiny, black, wiry stems. The fertile fronds may become quite tall (30 cm, 12''), with pairs of pinnae up the rachis, each one a bit smaller. The pinnae have about four pairs of more or less triangular pinnules, the lower ones often with "ear lobes," so they are arrowhead shape—an interesting and different form.

The sterile fronds have fewer pairs of pinnae and are never as tall. The margins of those pinnules are finely serrate.

This fern is an excellent and lovely houseplant, giving somewhat the appearance of the Maidenhair but demanding far less humidity. Small plants (which are available in most nurseries) are excellent in terrariums or grouped with miniature ferns.

Use a good humus potting mix with additional sand and oyster shell. They are alkaline-lovers and also need to be on the dry side of moist. So, don't water until the soil is just barely moist or almost dry. The extra sand will help that situation. Fertilize regularly every two weeks all year with one-fourth strength liquid organic fertilizer. As houseplants, little croziers will keep on developing if fertilized. Not suitable for outside since it is semitender and also because the stems are so brittle.

MAIDENHAIR CLIFF BRAKE (30%)

Green Cliff Brake
Pellaea viridis var *viridis (P. hastata)*

ST   This is another delightful variety of *Pallaea viridis;* the pinnae are smaller but more numerous than var *macrophylla,* producing a more delicate-appearing plant. It is an attractive fern with smooth, wiry, black stalks. The short sterile fronds have small, finely serrated pinnules. The taller fronds are fertile.

An excellent houseplant, it produces new croziers all year if provided with lots of light and kept regularly fertilized with one-half strength liquid organic fertilizers every two weeks. Use good potting mix with extra sand for drainage, and add oyster shell. *Pellaeas* like enough water, but soil should be almost dry before rewatering.

The stems of the tall fertile fronds are quite brittle, so tie them to slender stakes as they develop.

GREEN CLIFF BRAKE (30%)

Hare's Foot Fern
Polypodium aureum var *areolatum*

The Hare's Foot Fern is a striking, very easy-to-grow fern with large, golden-brown, furry-appearing rhizomes that creep over the pot or basket. They are much bigger and more colorful than the rhizomes on most ferns. The blue-green, leathery fronds may grow to be 30-75 cm (12-30'') long and 25 cm (10'') wide, so plan on giving it plenty of space. The wavy-edged segments of the frond are not quite divided to the midrib (a characteristic of many Polypodys). This is a good example of a pinnatifid frond.

E
T-ST

It is a marvelous plant in a hanging basket or pot in a high light spot—exotic-appearing in an office or home, yet easy to care for. It can take some winter sun, diffused sun in the summer. Be sure the container drains well. This fern likes rich soil, so use commercial mix with additional peat moss and sand or the rich fern mix. In the warm months water it so the soil is kept moist but not soggy; in winter it shouldn't be watered till the soil is almost dry.

Fertilize this excellent largish house fern with liquid organic fertilizer at one-fourth strength every month. The

HARE'S FOOT (20%)

fronds tend to keep uncurling all year if fertilized regularly. Old fronds will separate from the rhizomes with a clean scar when they become old.

Put this fern in fairly shallow pots or baskets, for they are top-of-the-ground rooters. Never bury the rhizomes. It is easily divided or started from rhizome cuttings at any time (see Propagation). Also easily raised from spores.

Victorian Brake
Pteris ensiformis cv Victoriae

E
ST

Victorian Brake is another small fern producing two very different fronds. The fertile fronds rise from the center of the clump and are tall with narrow, slender pinnae in pairs. Because of their tallness and abundance, they overshadow the broader, far more interesting and beautiful sterile fronds. These sterile fronds are bi-pinnate near the base, one-pinnate above with finely serrate edges and noticeable side veins—especially on the underside. Along the midvein of the sterile fronds (and somewhat of the fertile fronds) are whitish bands.

VICTORIAN BRAKE (25%)

The sori are arranged in a narrow line along the very edges of the slender pinnules of the fertile fronds.

This fern grows especially well in a terrarium—probably one of *the* best plants for a terrarium. It also does well in a shallow pot. Keep the soil evenly moist, and if not in a terrarium, mist occasionally. This is a clump-forming fern and can easily be divided by cutting through the many underground rhizomes (see Propagation), or move it into a bigger pot—at any time. It also produces quantities of spores and grows easily and fairly rapidly from them. Groom it regularly, and fertilize every month with liquid organic fertilizer at one-half strength; one-fourth strength in winter.

Downy Wood Fern
Thelypteris dentata (Dryopteris dentata)

This fern earns its name well, for the foliage not only looks soft, but it feels soft and downy. The mature fronds are

E
ST

DOWNY WOOD FERN (25%)

bluish or grayish-green and usually are at least 60-90 cm (2-3') long. The fronds and the individual pinnae are each long and tapering, the lowest pinnae often 7-8 cm long. The pinnules nearest the rachis on the lower side of most pinnae are much larger.

It is a semitender fern, lovely as an outside fern in protected, mild areas, with its graceful, soft fronds. It produces spores abundantly in a regular pattern on each pinnule (see print).

It is one of the easiest and quickest of ferns to grow from spores. The young plants, when given good care, also grow rapidly to mature size.

They like medium shady areas and abundant water. Fertilize them once a month with one-half strength liquid organic fertilizer to promote the full growth of the long fronds.

Semi-tender—nights not below 50°F . . . . ST
Semi-hardy—nights not below 35°F . . . . SH

Delta Maidenhair; Southern Maidenhair
Adiantum raddianum; (A.cuneatum; A. decorum)

The Delta Maidenhair seems difficult for some people to **SH-ST**
grow unless they have a greenhouse because of its demand
for high humidity. However, it can be a very successful terrarium plant. It also can be outside in pots in shady summer
patios in the humid east, and along moist shady walks in the
west. It is more delicate and harder to grow than *Adiantum
capillus-veneris,* but both, once established, do well.

The thin, wedge-shaped leaflets are more or less irregular-
ly incised and are on slender, wiry, branching black stems.
The fronds seem exceedingly delicate, and it is indeed more
exacting in its demands for humidity and temperature.

Fertilize only during the active growing period, and then
use only one-fourth strength every two weeks. Repot in late
winter if overcrowded, cutting off all old or damaged fronds.

DELTA MAIDENHAIR (20%)

Rosy Maidenhair; Australian Maidenhair; Rough Maidenhair
Adiantum hispidulum

SH-ST The Rosy Maidenhair is a different sort of Maidenhair, for the young fronds are rosy-pink, turning to a medium green when mature. The fronds are also quite harsh to the touch, though still appear quite delicate. The fronds are similar in shape to the Five-Finger Maidenhairs, with the slender dark stalk branching out in pairs to form three to seven pinnae; however, the basal pinnule is replaced by another, smaller pinna (see print). Each pinnule tends to overlap the next one. The slender black stem is rough with scattered whitish hairs—it feels like sandpaper.

This fern is an excellent houseplant (or outside in temperate areas), for it is more tolerant to low humidity and dryness than other Maidenhairs. Use north light or light from an east window if it gets no direct sun. Keep it moist but don't overwater, especially in winter. In fact, the soil should become dry between waterings.

ROSY MAIDENHAIR (35%)

Feed monthly with one-half strength liquid organic fertilizer during the growing season, none during the winter dormant period.

The sori are along the edge of each pinnule; as they ripen, the edge rolls in scallops over them. This fern is easily grown from spores, but more easily reproduced by dividing the clump with its fibrous roots (see Propagation). This can be done anytime, though best to do it when there are few new fronds, for they break easily. If you need to repot, do it in late winter before growth starts. Plant in good soil mix with additional sand plus limestone or oyster shells.

Mother Fern
Asplenium bulbiferum

Mother Fern is probably one of the best-known house ferns, and since it is semihardy to semitender, can be used outside also if you live where there is no frost. A protected patio or entry may be a good place for either a pot or a hanging basket. It likes lots of water but the soil must drain well. You can use regular potting mix, adding extra sand and peat moss, or the fern mix recipe, adding some perlite. Mother Fern does not need as high humidity as the Dwarf Mother Fern, but if your house air is very dry, a pebble tray may be useful. Be sure the pot does not stand in the water.

**E
SH-ST**

The attractive, evergreen fronds are a fresh, somewhat yellow-green color, the mature fronds tend to have a lot of substance but are not leathery. They are bi-pinnate, gracefully arching, and may be 25-50 cm (10-20'') long. The stalk and rachis becomes dark colored as the frond matures—an attractive accent. An immature plant will only produce sterile fronds—with broad pinnules, the margins scalloped or round-pointed. A mature plant will also produce fertile fronds, with narrowly lobed pinnules, intermixed with the wider, sterile ones—so an older plant has an interesting variety of fronds.

A fun characteristic that gives this fern its common name is the production of little fernlets on the upper surface of both sterile and fertile fronds. Little buds form which soon sprout tiny slender leaflets—often with scalloped edges. This budding develops on the Mother Fern when it is about a year old. At first, there will only be a few fernlets, but as the fern grows, more and more appear, eventually becoming very numerous and may seem to almost cover the fronds. (You'll know you're a success when this happens.) These can be carefully pricked off (or their attached pinnule can be cut off) and new ferns raised (see Propagation).

Mother Ferns do best in low light situations—north light is good. If the weather is hot and dry, they will benefit from some misting. Water regularly, so the soil stays evenly moist, but don't let it sog. If it outgrows its container, repot in late winter or early spring. Fertilize every two weeks with one-fourth strength liquid organic fertilizer.

MOTHER FERN (25%)

Hammock Fern
Blechnum occidentale

This is a smallish fern, somewhat similar to *Blechnum spi-* **E**
cant though the one-pinnate frond is shorter and varies more **SH-ST**
in width. It is a very colorful fern, for as the brown, scaly
croziers unroll, the young fronds show as a lovely coppery-
red, finally turning to deep green when mature. Fronds keep
unrolling all during the growing season, so there usually are
two or three pinkish or coppery fronds. The fronds may
grow to be 30-60 cm (1-2') long.

If small plants are available, this fern is good for terrariums. However, it will tolerate more dryness than many ferns
so don't put humidity-lovers with it—small *Polystichum setiferum* cv Proliferum is a good terrarium companion. It is
also lovely in a pot, for it soon spreads to make a dense mass
of fronds. It needs high light situations. Do not water it until
the soil surface feels dry. Planting mix should contain some
oyster shell or limestone chips.

They are also excellent ferns in gardens where there is no
frost. They will tolerate some morning or afternoon sun if
they have enough water. Filtered sun is probably best. Hammock Ferns make wonderful evergreen ground covers.

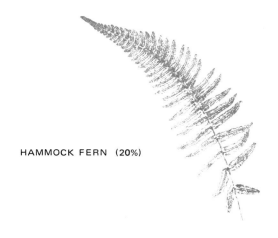

HAMMOCK FERN (20%)

Squirrel's Foot Fern; Rabbit's Foot Fern
Davallia trichomanoides

E
SH-ST

This lovely fern, available from shops most anywhere, goes by two common names—though Squirrel's Foot is used more frequently. (Rabbit's Foot is also the name used for *Davallia fejeensis* and *Polypodium aureum.*) Whatever it is called, this small fern is beautiful with soft-appearing, intricately cut fronds. They are thrice-pinnate-pinnatifid, up to 30 cm (12") long. The deeply cut fronds are roughly long-triangular in shape, shiny above, dull beneath, and are on slender green-bronze stems arising at intervals along the creeping rhizomes. These rhizomes are greenish, grayish, or tannish and scaly, and grow above the ground or creep along it. They are branching, and with their furriness, resemble animal's paws. New fronds continually unroll and expand along the various rhizomes during the growing season. During that period, fertilize every two to three weeks with one-fourth strength liquid organic fertilizer, tapering off during the three or four winter months. This fern may shed most of its fronds in late winter or early spring, leaving the furry rhizomes barren, but new fronds will soon start unrolling.

Squirrel's Foot is very easy to grow, and in mild winter areas makes an excellent fern outside on slopes and in rock gardens with its creeping, spreading rhizomes—a good ground cover. It also is especially lovely in hanging baskets in patio areas with the rhizomes forming an intricate pattern over the surface. Be sure it has good drainage. This fern is happiest if kept on the dry side of moistness—i.e., never water till soil surface feels dryish. It thrives in varied light conditions—from low to high. Although it does best if temperatures don't drop below 50°F, it can stand short freezing periods, though does drop its leaves then. It can stand drier air than many ferns and is therefore an excellent houseplant.

New plants are easily grown from rhizome cuttings (see Propagation) and from spores.

Bear's Foot Fern, *Humata tyermannii,* looks like a big Squirrel's Foot Fern, but the rhizomes are thickly covered with white furry scales. It makes good ground cover in temperate areas, and grows beautifully in baskets with same kind of care as the *Davallias.*

SQUIRREL'S FOOT FERN (40%)

Lace Fern
Microlepia strigosa

This beautifully lacy, light-green fern is a fast growing, **E** spreading species. It grows well outside in temperate areas; it **SH-ST** can take cold conditions if it is not too frosty for too long. It needs grooming regularly but produces beautiful masses of finely divided fronds which may be 1-1.5 meters (3-4.5') and 15-18 cm (6-8'') wide. Croziers keep unrolling during the long growing season. The long, tapering fronds are three-pinnate, the margins of the larger pinnules serrate. The pinnae are also long and tapering—a very attractive frond.

Lace Fern spreads rapidly by its creeping, hairy rhizomes, and can be divided easily (see Propagation). Do it in early spring, replenishing the humus so growth will continue to be full. This is an excellent fern to cover areas, and is easy to grow since it is not particularly demanding as to care or soil—just give it some fairly humus soil and water deeply, but only when the ground is almost dry. It does well in an east-facing situation where it is shaded by trees from the hot summer sun and although it likes lots of diffused light it also will grow well in less light.

Fertilize once a month one-half strength during growing season. Best planted in the ground. If in cold spots, leave old fronds on or add extra leaf cover to protect during the winter.

LACE FERN (40%)

Southern Sword Fern; Tuber Sword Fern
Nephrolepis cordifolia

This fern is a very common evergreen fern in gardens of the **E**
west. It is often sold as *N. exaltata,* but the bright green **SH-ST**
fronds are narrower and more upright. The pinnae are closely packed and even overlapping, and each pinna has an
"ear-lobe" at the base on the upper side which bends
backwards behind the rachis, and so shows as a flange. These
make an interesting overlapping pattern. The sori are abundant, usually on the upper half of the frond.

It spreads rapidly by the thin, scaly runners which produce
new plants at the tip. It also produces quantities of spores
and is an easy one to raise this way. However, the runners are
so numerous, that that method is easier and faster.

If you dig a clump of this fern, you'll find small, nut-like
or potato-like brown tubers along the rhizomes, used by the
plant for water storage. This fern will take cold temperatures
but not hard frosts. It is a sturdy fern for the garden, for it
does not require particularly good soils, can take various
kinds of shade, and even stands considerable periods of
drought. It is easily moved, most anytime. However, it seems
attractive to scale insects, so watch that (see Problems).

SOUTHERN SWORD FERN (20%)

Common Sword Fern
Nephrolepis exaltata

E
ST
The Common Sword Fern is not grown as often as *N. cor-difolia,* for it is not as hardy and sturdy. They are very similar, but the fronds of this fern are wider (15 cm, 6''), more arching, and longer (1.5 meters or more, 5'). It somewhat resembles the native Western Sword Fern, *Polystichum munitum* though the frond is narrower.

Plant in potting mix with additional sand. Fertilize every two weeks with one-fourth strength liquid organic fertilizer and groom regularly.

COMMON SWORD FERN (40%)

Australian Cliff Brake
Pellaea falcata

The Australian Cliff Brake is an excellent, smallish fern, **SH-ST** somewhat larger than others in this genus. The evergreen, one-pinnate frond may be 30-45 cm (12-18'') long, with 14-22 pairs of dark, shiny green, leathery pinnules. They are somewhat oblong, with a short tapered tip, heart-shaped at the base. The end pinnule is much larger, quite broad at the middle with a long, tapering tip.

This is a rock fern, preferring some lime in its soil. Use garden loam mix, adding oyster shell. It will take all the indirect light it can get but doesn't want much sun. It should be kept on the dry side—i.e., only water it when the soil feels almost dry. If in a pot, be sure water doesn't sit in the saucer. It does well in a hanging pot, for the fronds are long enough to drape gracefully over the container. Also excellent in a protected spot for a mass planting in the ground.

AUSTRALIAN CLIFF BRAKE (25%)

The sori are arranged along the very edge of the pinnules, usually more abundantly on the upper portion of the frond. It is easily raised from spores.

Fertilize with one-half strength liquid organic fertilizer once a month the whole year if a houseplant or outdoors in mild areas; if in cooler spots where growth slows down, feed just every other month during the colder weather.

BUTTON FERN (25%)

Button Fern
Pellaea rotundifolia

E
SH
When you first see this plant among ferns you can hardly believe it is one, for the frond of the many, little, round, leathery, very dark green leaflets seems very "unfernlike." It was given both its scientific and common name because of the shape of those leaflets or pinnae. It is one of the *Pellaea* genus, with wiry stems and sori around the under edge of the pinnae. There may be 20-40 more or less round pinnae alternately up the rachis, which is far more scaly in this species than in most of the others.

Many fronds develop from the branching mass of rhizomes, soon filling a pot or planter. It is a delightfully different and durable fern for the house, demanding less humidity than many. Small ones can be used in terrariums with other ferns that want to be on the dry side of moist, as

Blechnum occidentale, which also needs oyster shell in the mix. It is also excellent just as a potted plant in the house, in high light situations or outside in protected patios or entries where nights don't go below 35 °F. It is a semihardy fern, and does well in baskets, especially if hanging under lattice work or trees, thus getting the bright light it needs more than it would if on the ground. In the winter it can stand some sun.

Be sure that it drains well—don't let it sit in water. Use extra sand and oyster shell when fixing the potting mix. Fertilize every two weeks at one-half strength liquid organic fertilizer to keep the fronds continually developing. If the plant is outside where growth slows down during winter, taper off during that period.

This is an easy fern to grow from spores. It also divides well because of its numerous branching rhizomes. Divide in early spring, repotting in a fairly big container, for the rhizomes grow rapidly if given proper treatment. Don't fertilize for two weeks after repotting.

Gold Back Fern
Pityrogramma hybrida

A beautiful fern immediately noticed because the undersides **SH-ST** of its large two-pinnate fronds and the whole unrolling crozier are bright with a gold-yellow wax. This will rub off and is not the sporangia, though those also are colorful— green, black, and brownish orange, depending on their stage of development—and all don't mature at the same time. The young stalks are also golden but begin to turn darker when the frond is mostly unrolled. The stalk soon looses its scattered golden hairs, but the undersurface of the fronds remain yellow for some time, accented by the now shiny, dark brown stalk and rachis. The frond may be 25-30 cm (10-20'') long, the stalk not quite as long. The 10-20 pairs of pinnae are at first opposite, gradually becoming alternate and tapering as you go up the rachis.

The pinnules are regular, small lobed, the frond being a shiny, waxy-green on the upper surface. The fronds are upright or arching from a tight spiral at the end of the short rhizome. The sori are scattered along the veins, sometimes hidden by remaining "gold dust" on the undersides.

It is semihardy, so can be planted outside where the nights are no colder than 35 °F. If it is placed up on a wall or even in a high planter box, the gold back is more noticeable. Soil should be kept on the dry side of being moist, and it enjoys bright but not direct sunlight and medium humidity. It is also a good houseplant until it gets too big. It grows easily from spores.

Use a good fern potting mix and fertilize once a month with one-half strength liquid organic fertilizer. This fern is a cross between *P. calomelonos* and *P. chrysophylla.*

GOLD BACK FERN (40%)

Staghorn Fern
Platycerium bifurcatum

Staghorns are unusual, very different ferns. They are **E**
tropical epiphytes with two very different types of fronds. **SH-ST**
There are large, sterile "shield" fronds which are flat and
roundish or kidney-shaped, and form the base of the fern.
These turn tan or brownish as they mature; they are spongy
and their job is to hold water. There may be two or three
layers of them, eventually the older ones dying and rotting
away. The other fronds are green fertile fronds, and are long
and variously branched or forked. These generally hang or
stand outwards, growing from the center of the shield
fronds. The name comes from the common shape of the
foliage leaves, resembling horns. When mature, the undersides of the tips of these are covered with sori, making it look
as though they are lined with brown felt.

In the wild they grow on tree trunks (but not as parasites).
You can attach them to trees or have them on slabs of bark
or driftwood, outdoors if your area doesn't have temperatures much below 35°F, though the common staghorns can
even endure short periods of freezing weather. They also do
well indoors if they have plenty of bright, filtered light, have
good air circulation, and average to cool temperatures. They
prefer high humidity—mist if needed to reach about 50%,
but do not overwater. Staghorns are most successful if they
are not fussed over. Once established, they take only minimal care and too much TLC is deadly. They should hang in
good filtered light and not be crowded by close-by plants.
They can stand filtered sunlight in winter and bright shade
the rest of the year.

They should go dry between waterings. A good indication
is whether the moss below them is dry—if it isn't, then the
fern does not need watering. Another way to test (if the
shield is big enough) is to press your finger gently against
that spongy tissue. If it feels moist, it's fine—don't water
yet; if water drips out, it's already too wet. Don't be tempted
to water it anytime you water something else. In summer, it

probably won't need water more often than two times a
week; in cooler months, probably not more than once in two
weeks. If the plant is small enough to handle easily, it can be
watered by soaking in a tub or sink of water once a week.
Don't leave in more than fifteen minutes and be sure to hang
it up again immediately so the excess water can drip off.

Use one-fourth strength liquid organic fertilizer once a
month in summer, only every other month in cooler weather.
Liquid fertilizer is especially important in these ferns for
granules may lodge behind one of the fronds and burn it.

Platyceriums growing in pots should be vertically mounted
as soon as a nice-sized shield frond is formed and growth is
good. Overwatering is more apt to occur in pots, and as they
naturally grow on tree trunks or branches, their foliage
fronds show off better. This is easy to do—take a slab of
wood or bark, attaching a thick pad of sphagnum moss by
means of wires (not copper) or plastic tapes. On this pad
place the Staghorn so the foliage fronds can hang down, then
gently fasten wire or tape over the shield near its top and bottom. The plant should be held firmly on its pad.

Platycerium bifurcatum is the easiest Staghorn to grow. *P.
vassei (P. alcicorne)* is another easy one though it is tender.
P. bifurcatum cv Netherlands is a cultivar with darker green
fronds, but it is semitender. Several are quite difficult to
grow, but all must be kept on the dry side of moist.

STAGHORN FERN (20%)

California Polypody; Common Polypody
Polypodium californicum

There are several Common Polypodys in different parts of E
the world, and in many ways they are very similar— in- **SH-ST**
cluding the fact that they are common among rocks or on
bases of trees. They have long, hairy, knobbly rhizomes
which creep on, or just barely under the ground. They may
grow in loose woodsy soil or covered by an accumulation of
fallen leaves.

The fronds are very characteristic, for though they appear
to have separate pinnae, the divisions between the lobes are
not deep enough to reach the midrib. This is a good example
of what "pinnatifid" means—divided but not completely
separate. The fronds on this California species are numerous
along the rhizome. They usually are 7-25 cm long (3-10''),
the lobes with fine, saw-tooth edges.

The California Polypody, unlike many similar species, is
not really evergreen, but its best foliage grows during the
winter for it responds to the late fall and winter rains
characteristic of California. Except in moist creek or woods

CALIFORNIA POLYPODY (25%)

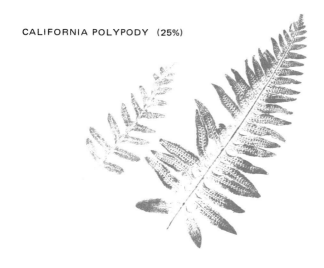

areas, you usually won't find fronds till after the first rains. Then you will see them unrolling on rocky ledges, on cliffs, and in woods, often in large clumps. The almost-round, very noticeable sori are large and bright yellow when mature, and are borne mostly on the upper part of the frond.

An easy-to-grow fern, easily transplanted and divided because of its branching numerous shallow rhizomes. Use good humus soil with quantities of leaf mold or peat moss. Watering during the summer will keep them producing fronds longer.

TABLE FERNS
Pteris

This is a very large group of mainly smallish ferns. The fronds are often forked or crested and frequently variegated, with the midvein areas whitish or silvery. The fertile fronds are usually much taller and more slender. They make excellent houseplants, partly because of their size which makes them suitable for terrariums or flattish pots, but also because they can stand night cooling to 50°F, though they prefer temperatures not below 55°F. Also, although they like to have moist soil, the fronds don't demand as much humidity as many house ferns do. They are all easy to grow, can take full shade or medium light conditions and will grow in regular houseplant mix, but do grow better with additional peat moss and sand.

E   Cretan Brake, *Pteris cretica.* There are many, many in-
SH-ST teresting and varied cultivars in this group. The basic frond
pattern is several fairly narrow, opposite pinnae, the lower pair branched or divided near its base into two similar parts. They are not minutely lacy ferns, but many are intricately divided or crested. Other species have whitish midrib areas. Fertilize every month with one-half strength liquid organic fertilizer during the growing season, gradually changing to

once every two months during the winter months. They are semihardy and will take occasional temperatures to 35°F, but prefer temperatures not below about 50°F.

Variegated Table Fern, *Pteris cretica* cv Albo-lineata. As the **SH-ST** name suggests, there is a broad creamy-colored band along the midvein areas of this medium green Table Fern. The pinnae of the fertile fronds are somewhat longer and more slender than the sterile frond. Also the edges of the sterile fronds tend to ripple or be wavy. It is an excellent house fern, and if fertilized with one-half strength liquid organic fer-

ALBO—LINEATA (40%)

tilizer once a month it will keep a good color but not grow too rapidly; fertilize every two months during winter. This fern will grow 30-45 cm (12-18'') tall eventually. Excellent in terrariums or dish gardens when small—move into larger pots as they grow. The sori are along the very edge of the narrow, taller fertile fronds, and become dark brown when mature. Divide the clumps whenever necessary (see Propagation). Additional peat moss and sand is useful if you use commercial house plant mix. Water enough so soil is evenly, but barely, moist, never wet. This fern can take weak winter sun and can be moved to a shady patio in the summer.

E
ST
The Parker Table Fern, *Pteris cretica* cv Parkeri, is a small fern commonly available in many nursery greenhouses. It has typical, simple, *Pteris* fronds with three simple, undivided pinnae, the tip pinna much larger than the others and each of the lower pair usually has a small basal lobe. The pinnae edges are finely serrate from about the middle to the tip. The side veins are very parallel to each other—notice the pattern in the print. The stalks are slender and green, with a definite rib on the upper surface. It is an excellent fern for terrariums for it stays small and compact.

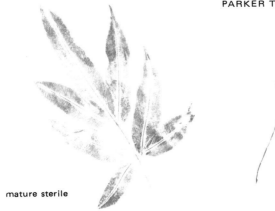

PARKER TABLE FERN (25%)

young fertile

mature sterile

Lacy Table Fern, *Pteris cretica* cv Rivertoniana, has the   **E**
typical, small oppositely branched fronds of the *Pteris*   **SH**
group, but the pinnae are wider in the middle and each is
more or less regularly and deeply lobed, the edges finely serrated. The narrow tips of some pinnae may also be divided
and somewhat crested. The plant indeed looks like coarse
lace. The slender stalks are green to brown. It is excellent for
planters and terrariums, for it remains small and in a close
clump. It can be divided by cutting through the clump if
necessary, but tends to grow slowly. As with other cultivars
in this group, prefers to be cool at night. It is semihardy and
likes to be moist, but be careful with its watering for since it
stays small, it tends to be in small containers and overwatering them is easy. If the container becomes crowded, they can
be repotted at any time, but don't move to too big a container. Keep the soil moist but not wet.

LACY TABLE FERN (70%)

E   Fan Table Fern, *Pteris cretica* cv Wilsonii. This bright green
ST cultivar has narrow pinnae, but the tips (especially of the
sterile fronds) become so divided and fringed that they
become fan-like and crested. The fertile fronds are not particularly crested. This fern tends to grow to be a much bigger
plant than either the Parkeri or Rivertonia cultivars.

E   *Pteris cretica* cv Wimsettii multiceps. This fern has fairly
ST small, flat fronds, with the pinnae intricately divided into
many linear lobes. The tips are fan-like and crested—producing a complex-patterned smallish clump. It is an unusual,
striking houseplant, good in a special display pot. It should
have low to medium light, moist soil (but not wet), and cool
nights (50°F).

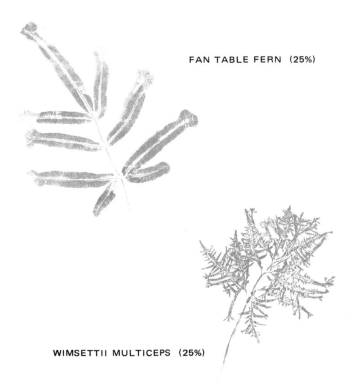

FAN TABLE FERN (25%)

WIMSETTII MULTICEPS (25%)

Pteris cretica cv Ouvrardii. This *Pteris* cultivar is a common **E** one found in nurseries and houseplant stores. It is somewhat **SH** similar to *P. cretica* cv Albo-lineata but it has no whitened areas. The frond is typically composed of three or more opposite pairs of pinnae, each gradually tapering and often curving slightly to the tip, the end pinna being much longer. Each of the lowest pair of pinnae has a similar pinna branching from it. The side veins are closely parallel to each other. The stalk is slender and tends to be quite long. This is a very easy container plant, increasing in size and height as time goes by. Move to bigger pots whenever necessary. Grows well in humus garden soil but additional peat moss and sand are helpful. Fertilize once a month with one-half strength liquid organic fertilizer. It also can easily be planted outside if in spots or areas where it won't freeze. Can stand some dryness and some sun, but does enjoy adequate water. It is a fairly tough fern with deep dark green fronds. Groom when needed, especially if it gets extra leggy. This is the easiest of the *Pteris cretica* cultivars to grow quickly to fair-sized specimens. It is good for cutting for flower arrangements.

OUVRARDII (30%)

Silver Brake; Silverlace Fern
Pteris argyraea (P. quadriaurita cv Argyraea)

E
SH-ST This beautiful, larger *Pteris* is a native of India. The fronds are lovely with a fairly wide band of silvery whiteness along the midvein of each long, tapering, somewhat bluish pinna. The pinnae are deeply divided or pinnatifid, each division with rounded tips. The lowest division of the paired basal pinnae is very much enlarged, forming a pinnule which also is deeply divided. These unusual pinnules tend to point down and out in a butterfly-like silhouette. Some of the other pinnae may have enlarged basal segments—all in all making a very attractive frond. The basal pinnae are always opposite.

The stalk is quite long and gradually becomes darker and has small scales near the base. The midvein groove extends

SILVER BRAKE (30%)

its length and is very noticeable. The Silver Brake forms a tight clump, new croziers unrolling from the center.

In mild areas it grows well outside—with fronds as much as 90 cm (3') long and 30 cm (1') wide at the base. In the house, it (hopefully) doesn't grow this large, but it is a bigger fern than most others in this group. It is an attractive fern, wherever grown. Start with a small one, moving its location and container to fit its size. It can be repotted at any time.

Plant it in a special fern mix or commercial mix with additional peat moss, sand, and a bit of bone meal. Outside plants can take some sun in the winter and filtered sun in the summer. Be sure it has plenty of light if indoors. Keep soil barely moist and be sure it drains well.

Fertilize only once a month indoors with one-half strength liquid organic fertilizer; outdoors every two months. If you want it to grow faster, cut the interval between feedings in half.

This fern grows especially well from spores. The sori are along the edges of the pinnae divisions, hidden by the curling edges, red-brown at maturity.

Pteris dentata (flabellata)

This medium-sized *Pteris* is somewhat similar to the Silver **SH-ST** Brake in the shape of its fronds, which are regularly and beautifully two-pinnate-pinnatifid, and has the typical pair of side branches off the lowest pair of pinnae. These trend out and down. The deep divisions are blunt-tipped, each pinna gradually tapering—a nicely shaped frond.

In protected areas and temperate spots this makes a beautiful outdoor plant, for it is semihardy to semitender. It needs medium light, likes moisture but adequate drainage. Fertilize once a month with one-half strength liquid organic fertilizer.

Ladder Brake Fern
Pteris vittata

E
SH-ST
This Ladder Fern is a "typical" *Pteris* with its long, narrow, opposite, regularly arranged pinnae, the lower pair branching at the base to form similar offshoots. The fronds are quite long—up to 75cm (30''), are very dark green and somewhat resemble some of the slender palms. It is an easy fern to grow both indoors or out in areas where it won't be frosted. It is a fast grower. It can stand some sun and enjoys lots of light indoors, but don't put it too near sunny windows, for that could burn the leaves. Keep soil evenly moist, not wet. Grow in rich garden soil with extra sand, and peat moss or perlite. Fertilize every two weeks with one-fourth strength liquid organic fertilizer.

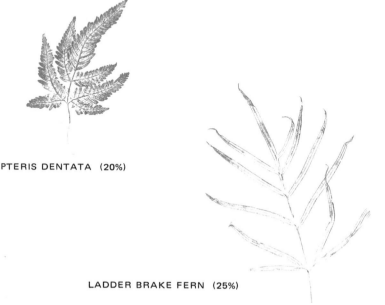

PTERIS DENTATA (20%)

LADDER BRAKE FERN (25%)

Australian Brake; Trembling Brake
Pteris tremula

Australian Brake is a large fern with attractive fronds which **E** may grow to be 1-2 meters (3-6') long. When small, it is quite **SH-ST** a yellow-green and can be used inside especially if you can give it morning or afternoon sunshine. New croziers unroll frequently, so it is a fun fern to watch. When it gets large, best to move it outside if it can stand your conditions. It is semihardy to semitender, so can take cool nights, but not freezing temperatures. If you can't move it outside, keep cutting the big fronds off (this helps to keep young fronds coming, anyway.) Older fronds tend to lose their yellow-green color and become almost bluish-green.

AUSTRALIAN BRAKE (50%)

next-to-lowest pinna

lowest pinna

It resembles the common Bracken in size and form, but is a much softer fern—not as rank or coarse. The fronds are two- and three-pinnate, each pinna, pinnule, and frond very uniform in pattern, and roughly long-triangular in shape. It is an attractive, quick-growing fern.

Use good humus garden soil plus some sand and bonemeal. It enjoys lots of water and needs some sun, especially in the winter; summer sun should be morning or late afternoon. Small young houseplants need a fair amount of humidity, so group with others or use pebble trays.

Although a clump fern, it develops other clumps readily; easy to divide by cutting between them with a knife. Fertilize once a month with one-half strength liquid organic fertilizer.

This is a native fern from Australia, New Zealand and up into India.

Leather Fern
Rumohra adiantiformis (Aspidium capense; Polystichum capense)

**E
SH-ST** Leather Fern is well-known to many people for it is so universally used in floral arrangements. It is raised by the thousands in Florida for its fronds, which are deep green, long-lasting, heavy, tough, and leathery, but appear fine and "fern-like" because they are two- and three-pinnate. The lower pinnae are three-pinnate, the pinnules deeply incised and serrated near the base, becoming less so near the apex of the pinnae.

Mature fronds are sturdy and do not wilt easily. There are many fronds in each bushy clump, with new fronds developing all during the growing season. The croziers are covered with thick, silvery hair-like scales, many of these persisting on the lower part of the stalk.

If kept in pots, the shiny fronds tend to be about 30 cm (12") long, but in the ground under ideal conditions they may become almost a meter long (3'). The frond is fairly broad at the base, the pinnae repeating that shape. It is lovely in hanging baskets, though particularly attractive if placed at the foot of steps or in pots where you tend to see it from above.

This semihardy to semitender fern is a sturdy one for gardens where temperatures don't go below freezing. Plant it in good humus or a growing mix with extra gravel added for drainage. It spreads from creeping and upright rhizomes, producing lots of fronds per season. Repot in bigger containers or divide in early spring if it gets crowded. Fertilize regularly every two weeks with one-half strength liquid organic fertilizer, and water only when the soil is beginning to dry. It likes medium to bright light and will take some sun if it is not too hot or too intense.

Cut the fronds as you want them for flower arrangements, and they will keep for long periods of time if just kept moist.

LEATHER FERN (35%)

TREE FERNS

Tree Ferns are true ferns, but are big plants developing large fronds rising from the top of a trunk. They are common in tropical areas and were abundant in swamps in past ages. Some species may grow to fifteen meters (40') in height, with fronds three or four meters (9-12') long. They are elegant specimens, some much more demanding of warm temperature, humidity, and space than others. Small ones are excellent in large pots in homes and offices where a dramatic plant is desired. In many protected areas, they can be grown outside. It's best to choose one for your spot that won't grow too tall. Some of the tree ferns, like the New Zealand *(Dicksonia antarctica)* and the Hawaiian *(Cibotium glaucum)* can be replanted when they get too tall by cutting them down and replanting the shortened trunk. To do this, first wrap the trunk, above where you want to cut it, with a thick, wide bandage of moss. Keep this moist, and if you're lucky, roots will develop from the trunk and grow into it. After several months, cut below this pad and replant the upper portion. Be sure soil is rich with humus, and has lots of sand for drainage. Keep it more moist than normal for a bit. The Australian Tree Fern will not develop trunk roots.

NEW ZEALAND TREE FERN (20%)

New Zealand or Tasman Tree Fern
Dicksonia antarctica

This tree fern is desirable in many situations for it is of **E**
medium size, generally no more than 3-5 m (9-15') tall. It **SH-ST**
doesn't grow as tall or as quickly as the Australian Tree
Fern. It is semitender to semihardy, so can stand temperatures to near freezing or below (but not for long); best to
grow it in a protected place. They do well in cool, shady,
nonwindy areas. They need soil containing peat and humus
and is well-drained. Sand should always be added; firbark or
redwood bark on the soil helps retain moisture.

The numerous, arching fronds grow to be 2 m (6') long
and 45 cm (18'') wide. The numerous shiny green pinnae are
slender and tapering, the pinnules regularly and fairly deeply
divided. The frond tapers rapidly at the tip, but gradually
from the middle to the base—thus the frond is far wider
from midway to tip than the lower portion. The lower pinnae
are progressively shorter and much more widely spaced; the
upper ones are crowded.

The long, green and/or brown stalks are roughish but not
scaly. The base of the stalk and the trunk are covered with
long, silky dark brown hairy scales. It thrives where the light
is good—high to medium, and can take diffused sunlight if
not too hot. Water it well; wetting the trunk helps keep it
moist, but don't keep the crown wet. It can stand drier days
if deeply watered. Fertilize once a month with one-half
strength liquid organic fertilizer during the growing period
when the croziers are unrolling.

If you live in colder areas and are growing this tree fern in
a container, you can keep it in a lighted basement, garage or
cooler bedroom during cold months. Do not fertilize it and
water only as soil approaches dryness. It can stand fairly low
temperatures. It prefers coastal, cool, but humid areas.

Dicksonia squarrosa is the Slender New Zealand Tree Fern;
it is similar in its requirements, except it is more difficult to
grow.

Australian Tree Fern
Sphaeropteris cooperi (Alsophila australis)
(A. cooperi)

E
SH-ST

This is a fairly large tree fern, and the one most commonly grown. It does well outside in temperate areas and as a young plant can be grown inside, but it soon gets big! It may span 6-7 meters (18-21') and grow equally as high. It needs a high light situation and will grow with some direct sun. It is semitender to semihardy and can stand short periods of freezing or frosts, but does not do well where it is windy. It is very easy to recognize because the stalks and rachises are covered with large, rough, tough golden-brown scales. The scales on the trunk are even thicker and rougher—all of them may be irritating to the skin—not a pleasant fern to work under until it grows tall enough.

They drop copious quantities of spores—often making the soil brownish-gold under them. Easy to raise from spores, but prepare for the space they're going to require.

The fronds are wide and large, more or less triangular in shape, definitely bigger in all dimensions than the New Zealand Tree Fern, and much faster in growing. The fronds tend to arch when the tree is young, but in older trees, the fronds extend more horizontally, producing an almost flat-topped silhouette in the garden. These are excellent under taller trees, and the ferns then produce shade for plants under them. They require good rich soil; add sand or small gravel if necessary for drainage. Water deeply and well, including getting the trunk wet (but not the tip). Fertilize once a month during spring and into early fall with one-half strength liquid organic fertilizer.

AUSTRALIAN TREE FERN (tip) (30%)

HAWAIIAN TREE FERN (30%)
lower pinna

81

Hawaiian Tree Fern; Hapu
Cibotium glaucum (C. chamissoi)

ST   This tree fern is usually available as a piece of trunk with perhaps 1 or 2 expanding fronds. The fronds grow to be 1-2 m (3-6') long. The stalks are covered with silky gold hairs, much finer and softer than the harsh, tough ones of the Australian Tree Fern. It is easily grown from spores.

It can be planted in a pot with planting mix and additional sand, or may be grown in the ground with good humus soil and adequate drainage in temperate areas. Or it can be put in a container and packed with enough pebbles to hold the trunk upright. It may do well for years like this if kept moist and fertilized regularly (one-fourth strength every two weeks). If in potting mix or the ground, fertilize with one-half strength every month during growing season, then just once during remainder of year.

In a mild climate it can be outside, though it doesn't want night temperatures below about 50°F. More often it is grown inside in a large container. It should be kept moist, but not constantly wet, and when not actively growing the soil should be just barely moist before rewatering.

The trunk was baked by Hawaiians and used as a starch substitute for taro and sweet potato.

Mexican Tree Fern
Cibotium schiedei

ST   This tree fern is similar to the Hawaiian Tree Fern but the fronds appear softer. It may be available as a trunk specimen, and can stand a drier situation than the Hawaiian. Unlike the other tree ferns, it produces shoots from around the base of the trunk. With care these can be removed and a new specimen started. It does not like night temperatures much below 50°F.

Semi-Hardy—to 35°F.......................SH
Hardy—to 10°F...........................H

Southern Maidenhair; Venus Maidenhair
Adiantum capillus-veneris (A. chilense)

Maidenhairs are some of the loveliest and daintiest of ferns, **E**
but they all like shade and ample humidity, and not all are **H-SH**
easy to grow. Some of them are extremely hardy, others really need the even temperatures and the humidity of a greenhouse. They are also lime-lovers. Some of them can be very successfully raised in your home or garden if you watch conditions carefully. All need to be protected against slugs and snails if grown outside, for these ferns have very tender foliage.

The Southern Maidenhair is the common, elegant Maidenhair Fern that is a native of many parts of the world. The thin fronds are a dainty, light green, with slender, branching pinnae, the veins radiating (rather than the usual midvein and side veins). The slender stalk and rachis are black and glossy, the whole slender frond delicate in appearance. In most temperate situations they may remain green all winter and can stand some drying during the summer, but then of course, they would turn brown.

Maidenhairs grow naturally in limestone areas, particularly enjoying cliff spots near waterfalls or springs. Anyone who has travelled through the Grand Canyon on the Colorado River has seen fantastic displays of this species around every spring and side canyon waterfall. The fronds may be just a few centimeters long or up to 30 cm or more (12''), arching or draping gracefully. New fronds continue to unroll all during the growing season from the horizontal rhizomes in and among the older fronds. Snip off the dying ones at ground level as they brown and wither. If you are growing them outside where it is cold enough for them to turn brown in the winter (or at least most of them), you may want to cut off all the fronds before the new ones start uncurling in the burst of spring growth. The sori develop around the edges of the deeply cleft pinnules, protected by the rolled edges.

They grow well outside in the right spots—better than inside unless you particularly watch the humidity. Choose a spot where they will get little or no wind or draft. Dryness of the air can be overcome on especially hot days by sprinkling with fine spray. Be sure the soil has enough sand to insure drainage and oyster shell for lime. Occasionally deep soak to leach soil of any undesirable mineral build-up. Maidenhair can stand a fair amount of winter temperature down to 28 °F.

They can be lovely as a houseplant, for their temperature range is suitable, but they do demand high humidity (50%), so pebble trays or terrariums are successful spots for them. Bathrooms are often a good location, for they tend to be more humid; otherwise, mist them occasionally. They like low light (north window). The soil always should be dampish

SOUTHERN MAIDENHAIR (35%)

(but not soggy). During the winter months they are not actively growing, so watch the watering. They will need less, but this will depend on the dryness of the air and the warmth the house. They can then adapt easily to an outdoor shady moist spot in the summer.

Maidenhairs are easily divided anytime, but best in late winter or early spring (see Propagation). When repotting, be sure not to use too large a container. Use package mix with extra sand and limestone or the recipe under Growing Mixes.

Feed every two weeks with one-fourth strength organic liquid fertilizer, except during the winter, nongrowing months. Groom regularly, especially in early spring, and repot when it gets too crowded.

Holly Fern; House Holly Fern: Fishtail Fern
Cyrtomium (Aspidium) falcatum

This deep green, leathery-leafed fern is a native of Japan. **E** Each evergreen pinna is large—they may be 7-10 cm (3-5") **H-SH** long, and 2-3 cm (1") wide. The edges are more or less toothed, and have a long tapering, curving apex. The fronds may grow to be 30-60 cm (1-2') long. In temperate areas it is excellent either indoors or out, and can stand temperatures to 35°F. Holly Fern needs cooler temperatures than many ferns (50°F) at night, so they can do very well in houses where the heat is turned down at night—or in cooler rooms. It prefers to be barely moist and will stand short dry periods; it needs to be watered regularly, but not too often. Holly Ferns also require low humidity and low light—all features useful in a houseplant. They can benefit by being moved outdoors in the summer—to a shady spot with good air circulation which helps to keep the humidity low.

It is a sturdy fern, growing as a compact clump—beautiful in a pot or in a garden spot. Always be sure, when repotting

HOLLY FERN (35%)

or setting it in the ground, to keep it as high in the ground as it was. The growing tip must not be buried.

Fertilize houseplants every two weeks with one-fourth strength liquid organic fertilizer. Outside plants should be fertilized every month during spring and summer, tapering off in the fall and not at all during the winter. Start again in the spring. Repot overcrowded ones in early spring. Use a good fern mix, with some extra sand or perlite for drainage. The mixed fir bark recipe is especially good for this fern.

Rocheford Holly Fern
Cyrtomium falcatum cv Rochefordianum

Rocheford Holly Fern has even more beautiful holly-like **H-SH** fronds than the main species, *Cyrtomium falcatum*. Each shiny green pinna is large, 10 cm (4'') with wavy, sharply toothed edges and lovely tapering, curving tips. The stalk is long, each frond with 7-11 pinnae.

This evergreen fern is an excellent houseplant for it is very durable. Keep it regularly watered but on the dry side (soil should be dry before each watering). It can stand short periods of being dry. It likes medium light, and prefers cooler temperatures and lower humidity than most ferns. It also does well outside if the temperatures are usually above freezing—protected patios are excellent spots.

Use a good humus mix, adding extra coarse sand for drainage. Fertilize with one-fourth strength liquid organic fertilizer every two weeks until late fall, then taper off.

This fern grows easily from spores or you can divide it in the early spring when the plant gets too big, or move it to a bigger pot.

ROCHEFORD HOLLY FERN (20%)

Coastal Wood Fern; California Shield Fern
Dryopteris arguta

E
H-SH

There are many species in the *Dryopteris* genus and they probably are the commonest ferns seen. *Dryopteris arguta* is the Wood Fern frequently found in the Pacific States from Alaska to southern California in both the coastal mountains and the Sierra Nevada. It grows in the humus, loose soils of rocky, partially shaded slopes, and is especially abundant in the fog belt. It forms an open, upright clump, the many fronds rising from stout, creeping rhizomes. The fronds may be 30-90cm (1-3') tall, with short, scaly stalks. The fronds are twice-pinnate (or almost) and will be 15-25 cm (6-10") wide. The oblong pinnules are fairly serrate.

This Wood Fern is an easy-to-grow species for the garden, flourishing in woodsy soil, given medium shade and some rough gravel to provide good drainage. It stays green all winter if it is not too cold. Some spring and summer fertilizing makes a lush plant—use liquid organic fertilizer so as not to burn the croziers. It can stand a fair amount of dryness and must not be kept too moist. Water deeply at regular intervals, but allow the soil to be fairly dry before rewatering.

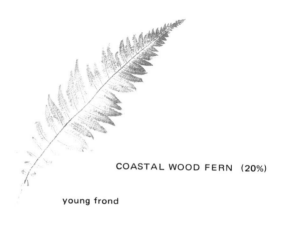

COASTAL WOOD FERN (20%)

young frond

Shaggy Shield Fern
Dryopteris atrata (hirtipes)

The Shaggy Shield Fern has deep green, almost plastic-appearing once-pinnate fronds 30-45 cm (12-18'') long. The **E H-SH** pinnae are regularly incised, with squared-off lobes between the incisions. The lower few pairs of pinnae turn downwards, others are at a right angle to the hairy, brown rachis. The stalk is even more hairy-scaly, the cluster of unrolled croziers in the center thickly covered with brown parchment-like scales. Young fronds are quite yellow-green, slowly changing to the deep forest green of the mature fronds.

It grows as a tight clump; be sure when planting that the crown is slightly above ground level. Excellent in the garden or in a pot outside—not particularly a houseplant except when young in a cool room. It wants no direct sun but needs good light. Grows well in the fern potting mix with fine fir bark. Soil should be almost dry before it is watered again, and it does not like water on the fronds. Fertilize with one-half strength liquid organic fertilizer once a month.

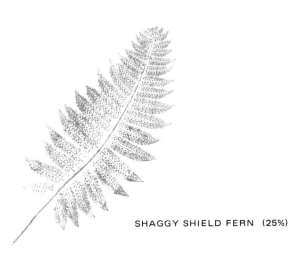

SHAGGY SHIELD FERN (25%)

Dwarf Leather-Leaf Fern; Tsusima Holly Fern
Polystichum tsus-simense

E
H-SH

This is a small fern with heavy, leathery, very dark green two-pinnate fronds. It is not really a miniature, but the fronds usually only grow to 30 cm (12'') long and 12 cm (5'') wide. The pinnae in this species are divided into pinnules, each with an incurved tannish small bristle. The basal pinnule on the upper side of each pinna is enlarged—like the "ear lobe" typical of many *Polystichums*.

It is an adaptable, easy fern, for it is hardy to semihardy, makes an excellent houseplant if kept cool enough, yet does well in a terrarium (60-70°F in the daytime). It should be given medium to low light conditions (no direct sun), requires moist/dry treatment, so shouldn't have water till the soil surface is almost dry, and will tolerate short periods of complete dryness. It must have good drainage; use houseplant mix with added humus and sand or your own mix. Fertilize only every month with one-half strength liquid organic fertilizer.

The croziers are covered with long white scales. The stalk has many golden hair-like scales, extending and scattered along the rachis. The whole pinna develops rust-brown sori in a single row on the underside around each pinnule. It grows easily from spores. The young sporlings develop amazingly long roots very early, but are a bit touchy about being transplanted.

Tsusima Holly Fern is a native of Japan and China and resembles Braun's Holly Fern, a native of the eastern United States.

DWARF LEATHER-LEAF FERN (65%)

Tassel Fern; Bristle Fern
Polystichum polyblepharum (setosum)

E
H-SH

Tassel Fern is a marvelously deep green, lacy fern with shiny fronds up to 60 cm (2') long. The pinnae are arranged at an angle to the rachis, each divided into 7-10 pairs of pinnules, which have bristly tips. Mature fronds are quite broad in the middle portion, then taper gradually to the tip—much wider than *Polystichum setiferum*. The lower pairs of pinnae tend to point downwards, and typically, the first pinnule on the upper side of each pinna is larger. The rachis in somewhat brown-scaly, especially in the lower portion; the stalk is densely so, the scales becoming quite large near the base.

This hardy to semihardy evergreen fern is excellent in gardens where there may be short periods of temperature below freezing, though it prefers above freezing temperatures. It does well in pots in protected spots and stays luxuriant throughout the seasons.

Plant in rich fern mix; some additional perlite is helpful. It enjoys bright diffused light but will tolerate a fair amount of shade. Water only when the soil has become slightly dry. Fertilize every month in spring and summer with one-half strength liquid organic fertilizer, tapering off in the fall.

TASSEL FERN (25%)

upper surface

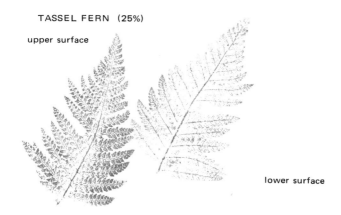

lower surface

Hardy—nights to 10°F . . . . H
Very Hardy—nights to -25°F . . . . VH

Five-Finger Fern; Common Maidenhair; Hardy Maidenhair
Adiantum pedatum

This delicate-appearing fern is actually one of the hardiest of ferns. It will stand freezing and, if well-mulched, it will become dormant and can take winter temperatures of -35°F. The shiny, dark, purplish-brown or blackish wiry stems divide into two recurving branches. From these there are three to seven pinnae (or more), with small, oblong, thin pinnules. This forms a fan-shaped or hand-shaped frond that spreads out, usually parallel to the surface. The fronds may be 25-60 cm (10-24'') long, 10 cm wide (4'').

During the growing season, the fronds continue to rise among older fronds, all along the creeping rhizomes. Once established, the Five Finger Fern continues without much

FIVE FINGER FERN (25%)

care if given adequate water. Don't water until the soil is dryish (but don't let it wilt—the fronds will not recover). It definitely flourishes in cold climates and doesn't do well where it is too warm.

It grows well in niches of limestone rocks or along concrete walks or ledges (this slowly provides it with the necessary lime). It wants abundant light, but not direct sunlight. If you grow this fern inside, keep it in a cool room.

If you use potting soil, additional sand, peat moss, and oyster shell are needed or make your own (see Growing Mixes). Fertilize with organic liquid fertilizer one-half strength every month during growing season. This fern spreads slowly, but can be divided (see Propagation). It is wise to do this before the new growth begins—either late winter or early spring. Groom the plants by cutting off all fronds (especially the outside ones) before the spring burst of new growth.

ASPARAGUS FERNS

E These are not true ferns, though they appear "fern-like" and are moisture-lovers. They produce flowers and berries, not spores. However we include them here for they are popular foliage houseplants (can also grow outside in areas with little or no frost), and are usually called ferns and sold along with true ferns.

They are fast growers with many branches, and are quite tough, for they can stand amazing periods of drought, and although they may not look too well, they'll recover. They respond to plentiful water, including misting, but the soil should just barely be kept on the moist side, and must drain well.

Because they grow rapidly, Asparagus Ferns must be fertilized regularly with one-half strength organic liquid fertilizer every month. They can be repotted any time of year, and if you add 1 ½ teaspoons 20% superphosphate and 2 teaspoons of 5-10-5 fertilizer and 1 tablespoon ground limestone, they'll be a really luscious green.

Usually plants that are bought from nurseries are rootbound. They should be repotted with fresh, good, potting mix with additional peat moss or bark in a larger pot. Several of the species are very attractive in hanging pots, though there are some forms that are upright and plume-like.

Asparagus Ferns must have adequate light; *Asparagus setaceous* and *A. densiflorus* cv Sprengeri can take some sun.

Sprenger Asparagus, *Asparagus densiflorus* cv Sprengeri is **H** the most common Asparagus Fern. The leaves look like small, yellowish-green flat needles. It produces tiny, pink flowers and orange-red berries. It tends to be pendant, so is excellent for hanging pots. It is hardy, can stand sun and drought amazingly well. Some sun, especially in the winter, is better for it. Well-suited to patios.

SPRENGER ASPARAGUS (20%)

SETACEOUS (20%)

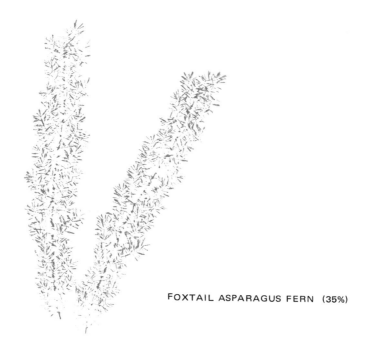

FOXTAIL ASPARAGUS FERN (35%)

H *Asparagus setaceous (plumosus)* is another common species, with feathery, flat, very dark green leaf sprays in tiers. It can become very leggy unless you provide some way for it to climb or keep it trimmed. It can take sun and is tolerant of some drought. Too little light or too much water makes it turn yellow. It is often used in floral arrangements.

Foxtail or Plume Asparagus, *Asparagus densiflorus* cv Myeri has stiff, upright stems with closely radiating tiny "needles," somewhat resembling a miniature bottle brush. It's a unique plant and certain to attract attention. It has small white flowers and red berries. It is excellent in a container, but must have very well drained soil—use plenty of sand in the mix.

Ming Tree, *Asparagus retrofractus,* is an unusual and interesting Asparagus Fern with a bonsai-appearance with its tiny leaves in tufts on erect, slender, zigzag stems.

Lady Fern; Glade Fern
Athyrium filix-femina

This fern has been called "one of the loveliest of the larger **E**
ferns," and one of the most widely spread. It grows naturally **H**
in moist forested areas, open brushy slopes, often in swampy
areas, drainage areas, near waterfalls, or in rocky areas—
wherever there is enough moisture in most parts of the
world. It is common in both eastern and western United
States.

It is very lacy-appearing, with the fronds twice pinnate, the
pinnules shallowly or deeply toothed, the edges appearing
finely fringed. It varies considerably with habitat.

Lady Fern is one of the easiest ferns to grow outside. It is
deciduous, but if kept well-watered, will stay green until the
first frost, when it will start turning yellow, shriveling and
disintegrating over the winter. New fronds unroll from the
crown in the spring, but new croziers also continue to unroll
throughout the growing season. They droop backwards till
partly grown and are at first covered by red-brown scales
which soon drop off.

Lady Fern should be planted in rich, humus soil and must
be kept moist or will turn brown. It can tolerate full sun if
sufficiently watered, but also enjoys spots in full or part
shade with less water. This fern is very hardy and can take
winter temperatures to -35 °F, the new croziers rapidly
unrolling after the snow or cold weather has gone.

It is a clump-former, the 60-120 cm long (2-4') soft, light
green fronds unfolding spirally around the crown. If growing in open areas, the fronds tend to be narrow with reddish
stalks and rachis; if the clumps are in woods or near streams
the fronds may grow to 1 ½ meters (4½') long and 30 cm (1')
or more wide. The pinnae are opposite near the bases (where
they are smaller and widely spaced), then become alternate,
larger, and closer together from about the middle to the tip.

The stout rootstalk has large, rust-colored scales. Lady Fern spreads, but slowly. The sori are very abundant with a crescent-shaped indusium.

LADY FERN (25%)
fertile frond

sterile frond

Japanese Painted Fern
Athyrium niponicum cv Pictum

The Japanese Painted Fern is a colorful fern. Though most **E** ferns which show color do so only in the new fronds, this **H** fern has lovely wine-red or purplish tones in the rachis and the pinnae midribs. The color develops best if the fern is planted or kept in partial shade. However, it does not do well in either deep shade or too much sun. It likes a high light situation with filtered sun or some morning and late afternoon sun. It can stand some dryness, but not for extended periods.

This native fern of Japan is a vigorous grower and will spread, but is not particularly invasive. You can divide it easily by cutting through the branching rhizomes (see Propagation). It is best to do this in early spring before the new croziers have elongated, as they break very easily. It is also easily raised from spores.

JAPANESE PAINTED FERN (35%)

The fronds may grow to be 60 cm (2') long and 15 cm (6'') wide, though often not this large. The stalk and the rachis are about equally long. The pinnae are usually alternate, but they may be opposite; they are about the same shape as the gradually tapering whole frond.

Plant in good humus soil, adding some peat moss and sand. This fern enjoys being kept moist, and though deciduous, it will stay green late into the fall if you keep up the watering. New croziers unroll during all this time if there is adequate organic matter in the soil. Fertilize once a month during summer and early fall with liquid organic fertilizer, tapering off in late fall and resuming when spring comes. When the first croziers show in the spring, you could fertilize twice the first month if you want lush growth. Let the old fronds protect the plant during the winter, but remove them in the spring before the new croziers have elongated.

Deer Tongue; Deer Fern; Hard Fern
Blechnum (Lomaria) spicant

E
H
The Deer Fern is a striking, deep green, small to medium size evergreen fern. At first glance it resembles a compact, narrow-fronded Western Swordfern or Christmas Fern. It is a very healthy, hardy, beautiful fern for the outside in deep shady areas. The once-pinnate fronds are numerous, spiralling from the crown, usually standing erect. They are quite evenly narrow, 2-9 cm, (1-3½'') except near the tip and near the long-tapering base where the pinnae are small and roundish.

The fronds may be 15-100 cm (6-40'') long, tough and quite leathery. There are many pairs of pinnae (30-80), closely spaced. The fertile fronds, growing from the center of the plant, are somewhat similar, but are taller and the pinnules, though more numerous, are further apart.

DEER TONGUE (15%)

Deer Tongue is a hardy, outdoor fern which thrives in deep shade or low light areas. Keep moist, but be careful of overwatering. It will grow in temperate areas, but doesn't do well in warmer climates. Use a good humus soil and sand.

Covelle's Lip Fern
Cheilanthes covellei

Covelle's Lip Fern is a very different, yet attractive, fern— **H** one especially suited to rocky, drier areas. It is a native of California, Arizona, and New Mexico. The numerous, leathery fronds are unique in that the pinnules are little and round, closely packed together so the pinnae look as though they are compact triangles or clusters of bubbles, beads or polka dots. The upper pinnae are especially close together.

The fronds are 13-20 cm (5-8'') long, at the top of a much longer, slender, purplish-brown, brittle stalk. There are long, tiny, hairy scales all along this stalk (especially on the back side), becoming more closely spaced towards the frond.

It is a hardy fern, and also can stand extended periods of dryness—the evergreen fronds gradually curling, expanding again when the rains come. In the west with its winter rainy season, it often looks its best when the deciduous ferns have dried up.

COVELLE'S LIP FERN (35%)

undersurface

Plant in a rocky, exposed spot in almost any kind of soil, except ones with clay. It does not need rich humus. Water sparingly, though it will stay greener for a longer period of time, if it gets some moisture. Do not get water on the fronds. Occasionally you might give it some very diluted liquid organic fertilizer.

Autumn Fern; Japanese Red Shield Fern
Dryopteris erythrosa

Autumn Fern is a beautiful, hardy, medium-sized plant. The **E**
"fall-colored" fronds as they first unroll give it the common **H**
name. The color lasts for quite a while, but gradually the
fronds change from the cinnamon-copper color to a deep,
rich green. Fronds keep unrolling during most of the growing
season, so usually there is a reddish frond or two among the
others.

This fern grows as a clump with many fairly broad fronds,
each frond up to 75 cm (30") long. They are twice-pinnate,
the pinnules serrated. The lower pinnae tend to turn upwards, giving the frond an interesting tiered or three-dimen-
sional effect. The abundant sori are in two rows flanking the
midrib. When young, the indusium covering the sori are red-

undersurface

AUTUMN FERN (20%)

dish or magenta, hence the fern's other common name. When mature, the sori are round, large, brown and very noticeable. Collecting spores and growing this fern is easy (see Propagation).

Autumn Fern is hardy and will be evergreen even in colder areas if protected by planting near big rocks or trees. It is an easy fern to establish and maintain—and an excellent garden plant. It needs a rich, humus soil or prepared mix with adequate sand. It likes medium to bright light conditions and will tolerate some winter sun. It wants to be fairly moist but will stand short periods of dryness. A beautiful, useful, and pleasant fern planted in the garden or in an outdoor pot. This low-growing fern is native to the Philippines, Japan, and parts of China.

Male Fern
Dryopteris filix-mas

H   The Male Fern has deep, shiny green leathery fronds, usually just once-pinnate, but the blunt segments of the pinnae are deeply cut. It is not common to find it growing wild in our country anymore, but it is fairly common in Europe. It can be grown from spores easily.

This fern is deciduous in cold areas, but the sterile fronds may stay green in temperate areas, rising on stalks with long scales. The fronds are broad, lance-shaped, tapering to a sharp tip. They may be 30-60cm (1-2') long and 20 cm (8'') wide when mature. The pinna often are oriented horizontally in relation to the rachis, and so seem to catch and reflect light.

The Male Fern wants a shady place in rich humus. A garden situation with good drainage (deep rocky humus is best), with plenty of moisture. The new shaggy croziers form during the late summer. Heaping some compost over the clump will help if the weather is cold and dry for long periods. This fern does not spread—reproduce it by spores which usually mature in July or August.

Evergreen Shield Fern
Dryopteris intermedia

The Evergreen Shield Fern is not only very hardy, but also is **VH**
extremely beautiful with very finely divided, two-pinnate or
even three-pinnate fronds. Sometimes it is called the Fancy
Fern because of these intricate, long-lasting fronds, and is
often used in floral arrangements. The basal pinnae are important to notice, for this species is very similar to
Dryopteris spinulosa.

The fronds may be 30-90 cm (1-3') long, rising from a tight
clump with next spring's croziers already forming. The
clump sits high in the ground—so when transplanting be sure
not to bury it. It does not spread, but grows quite easily from
spores which usually mature in June. For lush fronds and to
encourage crozier formation fertilize once a month from
spring to midfall.

This common native fern of the east is found from Canada
to Alabama and west to Wisconsin and Missouri; in the
southern part of its range it is found mainly in the mountains. It is an excellent fern in gardens with deep humus that
is rocky enough to drain well. Requires lots of water but if it
has enough it can take some sun.

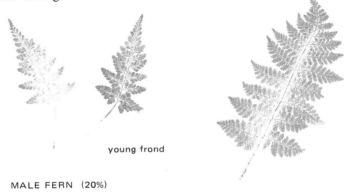

young frond

MALE FERN (20%)

EVERGREEN SHIELD FERN (25%)

Spinulose Woodfern
Dryopteris spinulosa

H   The Spinulose Woodfern is another lovely, lacy, fairly large, clump fern of the *Dryopteris* genus, common in woodlands from eastern Canada south to Virginia and east to Idaho. It produces a fibrous crown with many fronds arising from a tight spiral in moist woodsy areas with deep soil. One variety of this fern grows best in very wet areas.

The deep green fronds may be 60-120 cm (2-4') long, the lower pinnae may be 12-25 cm (5-10'') long.

Each pinna has many deeply cut pinnules which tend to be smooth-sided with the tips toothed. The first pinnule on the lower side of the basal pinna is usually longer.

This fern tends to be evergreen, especially if the winter isn't too severe or in more temperate areas. It is a hardy fern and excellent for the shady garden, or a north side, and is beautiful in clumps among rocks or logs or against a tree. It prefers slightly acid soil and wants lots of water.

SPINULOSE WOODFERN (60%)

Sensitive Fern; Bead Fern
Onoclea sensibilis

E   The Sensitive Fern is an easy-to-grow fern, and it can become
H   invasive if the conditions are right. The broad sterile fronds
have wide segments that seem to flow into the expanded
rachis except for the lower segments which are separate pinnae, often with definite stems. The edges of the segments are
scalloped or shallowly lobed. These sterile fronds are from
30-60 cm (1-2') tall, and are deciduous.

The fertile frond is very different, and it is persistent. It is
erect and looks like a stick with short strings of green beads
marked with brown lines. Each of these "beads" is really a
modified pinnule curled around several sori.

This common fern of southeastern Canada and the United
States to Florida and Texas grows in very damp or marshy
areas. Where there is plenty of water it can stand full
sunlight, but it will grow in almost full shade also.

SENSITIVE FERN   (25%)

Royal Fern; Flowering Fern; Locust Fern; *Osmunda regalis* var *spectabilis*

This very unusual, unfernlike fern has many common **H** names. It is often called Flowering Fern because the bead-like sporangia are borne in branching clusters at the tips of the fertile fronds—not on the undersides of pinnules as is the usual location. Also the fronds resemble Locust leaves—hence one of the names. They are two-pinnate, the pinnules quite broad. The fronds are 60-120 cm (2-4') long, but in perfect growing conditions may be 180 cm (6') long, very similar to some ferns in prehistoric swamps.

The sterile and fertile fronds are very different. The fertile frond has few pinnae (usually only two or three pairs) that are widely spaced. At the tip is the "blossom," made of three or more pairs of opposite branches, each with several short side branches. These side branches are really reduced pinnules, mostly just the midribs, bearing bead-like clusters of sporangia along them. When mature, these are in solid masses surrounding the midvein. The sterile frond has similar pinnae but there will be five or more pairs of them, fairly closely spaced, plus the tip pinnae.

Royal Fern is deciduous, and produces new croziers only at the beginning of the growing season, not all summer long as do many ferns. Transplanting is best done in early spring; even then be careful to not damage the croziers. The hairy brownish-wine colored croziers are prominent in early spring, changing to reddish green as they unroll. Before the fertile croziers completely unroll, the terminal green sporangia appear. The spores are green when mature for they contain chlorophyll. They must be planted as soon as possible after ripening, which is in late spring generally. After discharging their spores, these fertile tips turn brown but remain on the frond throughout the season.

This very primitive fern produces many fronds from the tip of an elongated rootstalk, typically forming a tussock. The black wiry roots grow in all directions deep in the ground. Over the years it spreads slowly from the center out.

It is a very hardy fern and is common in the boggy, swampy areas of eastern United States and northern Europe. It can be raised in the west if given the proper acid wet conditions. Be sure to give it extra peat moss and an excess of water. It will grow in sunny, semisunny to deep shade areas—the amount of light not as critical as the abundant wetness and the very acid soil requirement. Plant in boggy areas, along a stream or in low places in the garden where it can be constantly moist. It is a strong grower.

ROYAL FERN (35%)

Hart's Tongue
Phyllitis scolopendrium

A beautiful, bright green, simple-fronded fern that is **H**
especially lovely as a contrast to the more delicate, finely-
divided ferns. In color and shinyness, it resembles the Bird's
Nest Fern, but the fronds here are narrow, longish (20 cm)
and have rippled edges—''like a beautiful bright green Dock
plant.''

The base of the frond is heart-shaped (not the origin of the
name—a Hart is a deer-like animal). The main part of the
frond is uniformly oblong till the pointed or roundish tip.
Each vein divides soon after leaving the midrib, those veins
then parallel to each other. The sori are between pairs of
veins. The fronds are usually 20-45 cm (8-18'') long. If growing in very favorable spots they can even be longer, or if in
drier habitats may be only 4-5 cm long.

In its native habitat in the eastern United States, Great Bri-
tain, and northern Europe it is usually found on rocky,
shady banks in woods, usually near streams and definitely in
limestone soils. It has become rare in the wild. If planting it
in gardens, provide it with nearby limestone rocks or put
oyster shells in the soil mix. Give it shade and moisture, as
well as good drainage.

It is not truly evergreen, for individual fronds don't last a
full year, but new ones keep on unrolling. It is hardy and
does well in cold climates, but watch for slugs and snail
damage when the weather warms.

This fern is also a delight in the house, when young, or in
its own pot and spot when larger, preferably in a slightly cool
place. Fertilize every two weeks with one-fourth strength liquid organic fertilizer during the growing season. Water
regularly but not heavily and don't allow to sog; let the soil
become almost dry between waterings.

Hart's Tongue grows easily from spores and can be grown
by rooting the stalk (see Propagation). It is often especially

HART'S TONGUE (25%)

lush near pools. Add extra sand to a humus and limestone soil or use a good fern mix, increasing the sand or perlite ratio slightly. Be sure to add oyster shells or limestone chips.

California Gold Fern
Pityrogramma triangularis

E
VH This small fern grows on rocky, shaded but dryish slopes from British Columbia to Nevada and throughout California to Baja. It will thrive on amazingly little water, and when the rains stop, the fronds slowly curl up on themselves, new ones quickly growing with the return of the rainy season. The fronds of this fern, like *Pityrogramma hybrida,* have lovely, waxy, golden undersurfaces. The croziers are greenish-golden. Many small fronds, broadly triangular or almost pentagonal in shape grow from the rhizome on long, polished, brown stalks. The fronds may be 5-15 cm long and wide (2-5''), and are one-pinnate except for the larger basal pinnae which are two-pinnate.

The California Gold Fern is a reliable little rock garden fern which will tolerate considerable sun and dryness, but also responds well to richer soil and adequate water. Never water it, however, until the soil is dry. It can also be a very successful container plant, withstanding a lot of conditions most ferns won't live through—truly a beautiful little native. Fertilize it a couple of times during the growing season if you wish, with one-half strength liquid organic fertilizer. Use a humus garden soil plus considerable sand.

CALIFORNIA GOLD FERN (45%)

Christmas Fern; Dagger Fern
Polystichum acrostichoides

Christmas Fern is a common, well-named fern indigenous to the northern and eastern United States. It is a hardy evergreen fern, beautiful in the winter with its glossy, rich green, tapering fronds. The fronds are one-pinnate, each pinna having an ear-like lobe on the upper edge, and with more or less incurved prickles on the margin. It resembles the Western Sword Fern, *P. munitum,* which also likes to grow on rocky wooded hillsides or along shady streams. The fronds are often cut for bouquets or winter decorations, especially the varieties with very toothed pinnae.

E
VH

It is a very hardy fern growing from Nova Scotia to Wisconsin and south to Texas and Florida. It is easy to grow in deep humusy, but rocky, garden soils, preferably containing some lime. If kept moist enough, it can tolerate open shade to some sun, and is attractive year round.

The lance-shaped fronds may be 10 cm (4'') or more wide and form a clump 30-100 cm (1-3') tall. The two lowest pinnae turn downward and are opposite; the others stand out or trend upwards and become alternate. The lower half of the fertile fronds resembles the sterile fronds, but the upper, sori-bearing pinnae are noticeably smaller and narrower. The sori are round and very abundant, nearly covering the surface of those upper pinnae; the spores are ripe early in the summer. This fern is easily grown from spores. Fertile fronds are the first to unroll, rising from the center of the clump. Both fertile and sterile croziers are covered with silvery-gray, hairy scales.

CHRISTMAS FERN (20%)

Western Sword Fern
Polystichum munitum

E
H This Sword Fern is the common western evergreen fern with stiff, leathery, dark green fronds. It produces a heavy clump with erect fronds, or if on a steep slope they tend to arch gracefully, the lowest fronds seeming to flow down the slope. It somewhat resembles the eastern Christmas Fern, *Polystichum acrostichoides,* but the fronds may be thicker and more leathery—a truly excellent outdoor fern. The

undersurface

frond from young plant

fronds are one-pinnate, each pinna with a noticeable ear-like lobe on the upper side at the base and angled abruptly on the other side. The margins are serrate with incurved, small spines. Fronds on young plants always appear to be softer and more noticeably toothed. Pinnae are only slightly shorter at the base, with the upper third of the frond gradually tapering to the apex.

The sori are large, very round, and extend in a single row around the pinna, including the ear lobe. Usually only the upper part of the frond will produce sori, but it is not noticeably narrower as in the eastern Christmas Fern.

Western Sword Fern is found abundantly in damp wooded slopes from Alaska to southern California and in the northern Rocky Mountains. It is variable in form depending on habitat, and prefers shady, rocky but moist, humus soils. It will, however, tolerate some sun and will stand extended drought periods. It may loose fronds, but new ones will grow when watering is resumed.

This hardy fern makes an excellent deep green display clump in gardens or as background for other plants, and though native in the west, should do very well in the east. The fronds may turn wine-bronze as they age or when cold weather comes.

Soft Shield Fern; English Hedge Fern
Polystichum setiferum (angulare)

E
H

This is a beautiful evergreen fern with twice-pinnate fronds which are fairly narrow and appear very soft and feathery because the pinnules are small and deeply cut. When looked at closely, each pinnule seems to be shaped somewhat like a pointed glove—the thumb always next to the midrib, and each finger ending in a fine "thread" (not a bristle because it is soft and tiny). The frond is very long, the rachis and the very short stalk covered with thick masses of reddish-gold, hairy scales. Most of the pinnae stand out at right angles to the rachis.

Polystichum setiferum is considered by many to be one of the most elegant of the hardy ferns and many cultivars have been developed (see below). All of them are characterized by the production of fuzzy greenish-golden buds on the rachis at the base of the pinnae. These develop into fernlets with several tiny, divided fronds. They may be removed and planted when the little fronds are 1-2 cm long (see Propagation).

This low-spreading clump fern prefers shade but can take filtered sun. Grows very well in rich, humus soils with some limestone, and enough small rocks or gravel to provide good drainage. The soil should be just barely moist before it is watered again. It is hardy to 10°F and can tolerate long cold spells except when actively growing. If a late cold spell comes, give it some protection.

Fertilize from early spring until its growth slows down in the fall. Use one-half strength liquid organic fertilizer every month. Divide and/or repot in early spring. Do not fertilize newly planted ferns for two weeks. Use regular or rich fern potting mix, adding oyster shell.

SOFT SHIELD FERN (25%)

Japanese Lace Fern, *Polystichum setiferum* cv Plumosum, is a cultivar with super finely-divided and overlapping pinnae, the pinnules soft and tiny. Often available as a very small plant and then very useful and charming in a terrarium. Needs medium light. Put with other ferns that are not great water lovers, for this needs to be just barely moist before being rewatered. *Polystichum setiferum* cv Cristatum is another cultivar with overlappying, crested pinnae, the frond appearing almost fuzzy it is so fine.

Bracken
Pteridium aquilinum

E
H
Bracken is the most common fern in the world. With its numerous varieties, it is found almost everywhere. It grows in many different kinds of habitats—from moist woods and thickets to damp slopes to open fields and meadows. It may be a large, tall, rank fern (to 2 meters, 6') or be stunted and small in dry areas—less than 30 cm (1') tall.

The frond is very typical, no matter what size—bipinnate-pinnatifid to tripinnate-pinnatifid. There are one to four pairs of progressively smaller, opposite pinnae, then the upper part of the frond is just pinnate. The whole frond is roughly triangular, the lowest pinnae large and wide-spreading, almost as large as the rest of the frond. There is considerable variation in fronds. In some the pinnules are quite narrow with a short pointed lobe in between taller, rounder lobes, while other pinnules have broad and almost overlapping lobes (see prints).

The sori are borne along the edges, the indusium continuous with the curling or rolled-under edges of the pinnules. The spores are ripe in August and September and shed in quantities.

It can become very invasive, for the rhizomes are deep underground, branch freely, and grow rapidly. For this reason, it is also one of the first plants to regrow after a fire. In fact, it often crowds out other things following a fire or overgrazing. The fronds arise at intervals along the rhizomes.

The fronds of Bracken are not evergreen; they turn golden tan in the fall, but persist as dried, brown masses until the following year.

If you want a fern to "take over" this will do it, for it has few rigid requirements. However, it is a beautiful fern in its shape and intricacy of frond. The young fronds and rhizomes are edible if cooked.

BRACKEN (35%)
upper portion of frond

Chain Ferns
Woodwardia

E
H The Chain Ferns are a group of large, very beautiful clump ferns which are excellent additions to gardens. The sturdy fronds are one-pinnate-pinnatifid in a very characteristic pattern. The name comes from the end to end arrangement of the oblong sori, resembling links of chain, on each side of the midvein.

They seem to flourish in ordinary garden soil, if it drains well, though they grow far more lush in rich humus. They require lots of water but will live with moderate amounts, however, with less water, they don't grow as tall or produce as many fronds.

Chain Ferns are deciduous, but don't remove the old fronds until the following spring, for they are needed to protect the clump. They are hardy ferns but will thrive in temperate areas also. They like high light situations and grow especially well and luxuriantly under trees which give filtered light or along creeks.

Western Chain Fern, *Woodwardia fimbriata,* grows from British Columbia south through California and Nevada and Arizona, and is most luxuriant in the Redwoods. Its sturdy stalk is thickly scaly near the base, the scales becoming more and more spaced out till finally the upper rachis has practically none. It grows as a large clump, closely spreading by root buds. The fronds may be 1-2 meters (3-6') long, with 12-18 opposite (becoming alternate near frond tip), deeply divided pinnae. The chain pattern of the sori is very noticeable even on the upper surface. This is an excellent garden fern as a background for lower plants, and in the southern part of its range it may stay green (though not actively growing) through most of the year. Divide big clumps early in the spring; also easily raised from spores.

H Virginia Chain Fern, *Woodwardia virginica,* is a widely creeping large fern growing best in wet places, occasionally even standing in water. It only needs ordinary soil except that it must be very acidic. It will take very warm weather and full sun if it has enough water.

Oriental Chain Fern, *Woodwardia orientalis,* is not quite as **H** large-growing as the others. Its fronds resemble *W. fimbriata* except that the lobes are wider, longer, and more widely spaced. It produces hundreds of little buds on the upper surface of its fronds. These can be flipped off as soon as they have a couple of small leaves and planted (see Propagation).

European Chain Fern, *Woodwardia radicans,* is also a love- **H** ly, large fern with long fronds, producing a clump which spreads from the roots. It produces buds at the tip of the fronds. These can be anchored down until the bud develops roots and some small leaves, then the frond tip can be snipped off and the little plants will be independent.

CHAIN FERN (30%)

Glossary

ALTERNATE: Leaflets or pinnae at different levels up the rachis—not opposite

BI-PINNATE: Two-pinnate: Twice divided, the pinnae divided into pinnules

COMPOUND FROND: A frond that is divided into 2 or more leaflets or pinnae

CRESTED: The tips of the pinnae repeatedly forked

CROWN: Center of ferns with closely packed, unrolled croziers

CROZIER: The young, uncoiling fern frond; also called fiddlehead

CULTIVAR: A plant variety resulting from man-made crosses rather than one which occurred naturally. Written as cv., that portion of scientific name not in italics

ENTIRE: Referring to edge or margin of pinna or pinnule, meaning it is smooth

EPIPHYTE: A plant attached to another plant, but not parasitic

FERTILE FROND: The frond which produces spores

FROND: The leaf of a fern

INDUSIUM: The membranous or scaly covering of a sorus

OPPOSITE: The pinnae of a compound frond arranged across from each other up the rachis

PINNA (pl. PINNAE): A leaflet of a frond, the first division of a compound frond

PINNATE: Referring to a frond that is compound or divided just once

PINNATE-PINNATIFID: The frond first divided into pinnae, then the pinnae are deeply cleft, lobed, etc., but not clear to the midvein

PINNULE: The division of a pinna

PROTHALLIUM (pl. PROTHALLIA): The tiny plant produced by the spore. Usually heart-shaped; produces male and female cells which, when united, develop into the sporophyte plant—the plant we think of as a fern

RACHIS (pl. RACHISES): The midrib of the fern frond (above the stalk); especially used when talking about a compound leaf

RHIZOME: The horizontal stem of a fern, anchored by roots on underside; may be above ground or below the surface

SORUS (pl. SORI): Cluster of sporangia having a definite shape

SPORANGIUM (pl. SPORANGIA): The case which encloses the spores
SPORE: An asexual reproductive cell which may produce a new plant
SPOROPHYTE: The fern plant as we know it—the one that produces spores
STERILE FROND: The frond which is only vegetative, producing no spores
TRI-PINNATE: Three-pinnate: divided three times, pinnae divided into pinnules which are divided
VARIETY: A naturally-occurring, slightly different type of species—written var.

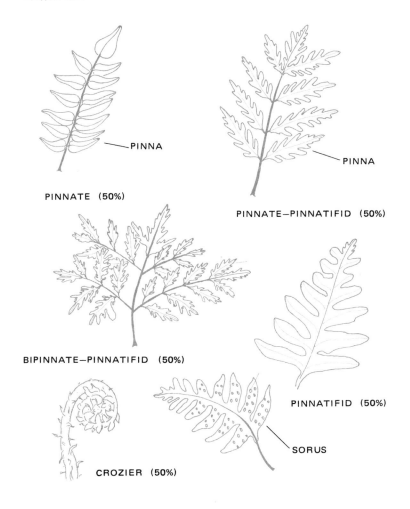

PINNA

PINNATE (50%)

PINNA

PINNATE—PINNATIFID (50%)

BIPINNATE—PINNATIFID (50%)

PINNATIFID (50%)

CROZIER (50%)

SORUS

Bibliography

Abraham, George, *The Green Thumb of Indoor Gardening.* N.J.: Prentice-Hall, 1967.

Abrams, LeRoy, *Illustrated Flora of the Pacific States,* Stanford, California: Stanford University Press. Vol. 1 1940, Vol. 2 1944, Vol. 3 1951, Vol. 4 by Roxana Ferris, 1960.

Brooklyn Botanic Garden, *Gardening with Native Plants,* Handbook #38. Brooklyn, N.Y., 1962.

Cobb, Boughton, *A Field Guide to the Ferns and their Related Families of Northeastern and Central North America.* Boston: Houghton Mifflin, 1963.

Crockett, J. U., *Foliage House Plants.* Time-Life Encyclopedia of Gardening series. N.Y.: Time-Life, 1972.

Foster, Gordon F., *Ferns to Know and Grow,* N.Y.: Hawthorne Books, Inc. 1971.

Gleason, Henry A., *The New Britton and Brown Illustrated Flora of Northeastern North America and Adjacent Canada,* N.Y.: The New York Botanical Garden, 1952.

Hoshizaki, Barbara Joe, *Fern Grower's Manual.* N.Y.: Knopf, 1976.

Kramer, Jack, *Ferns and Palms for Interior Decoration.* N.Y.: Scribner, 1972.

_____ *Natural Gardens; Gardening with Native Plants.* N.Y.: Scribner, 1973.

Parsons, Frances T., *How to Know the Ferns; a Guide to the names, haunts and habits of our Common Ferns.,* 2nd ed. N.Y.: Dover, 1961.

Sunset Editors, *Western Garden Book,* Menlo Park, California: Sunset, 1976.

White Flower Farm, *The Garden Book.* Litchfield, Connecticut: Fall, 1977.

Fern Societies:

American Fern Society
    c/o Smithsonian, Washington, D.C.

Los Angeles International Fern Society
    4369 Tujunga Ave., North Hollywood, California 91604.

Index

125

BOOKS OF RELATED INTEREST

WILDFLOWERS OF THE EAST by Mabel Crittenden and Dorothy Telfer is a complete resource for identifying local wildflowers in the eastern United States. Written in a clear, enthusiastic, and informative manner, it is illustrated with delicate line drawings and incorporates an easy-to-follow "key" for identifying individual plants. 224 pages, soft cover, $4.95

WILDFLOWERS OF THE WEST by Mabel Crittenden and Dorothy Telfer uses the same unique approach so successful in WILDFLOWERS OF THE EAST. "A joy to read" --- Sierra Club Bulletin. "Totally digestible" --- Sacramento Bee. "A delightful botanical guide to the identification of flowers that can be used by readers of every age... It is a gem." --- Booklist. 208 pages, soft cover, $4.95

TREES OF THE WEST by Mabel Crittenden again uses the same original approach that was used in WILDFLOWERS OF THE EAST and WILD-FLOWERS OF THE WEST. This unique guide will enable untrained observers to track down the family, the specific variety, and the family members of most trees they encounter. Although this carefully illustrated book focuses on the most common species in the Western states, the key can be used to identify the majority of trees anywhere in the United States. 224 pages, soft cover, $4.95

In THE HERBAL DINNER: A RENAISSANCE OF COOKING, Rob Menzies presents a unique, illustrated guide to understanding and using nature's herbal bounty as nourishment for the body, mind, and soul. The author draws on a rich blend of scientific fact and traditional lore in his discussion of planning and growing an herb garden; gathering, drying, and storing herbs; identifying medicinal herbs, and more. 224 pages, soft cover, $5.95

In DRIFTWOOD SCULPTURE: FROM DESERT, FOREST, AND SEA, Jean Thornber presents a beautifully illustrated, step-by-step guide to transforming weathered wood into dramatic works of art. "Makes use of natural materials and imagination in a unique way." --- San Francisco Examiner & Chronicle. 128 pages, soft cover, $4.95

Available at your local book or department store or directly from the publisher. To order by mail, send check or money order to:

Celestial Arts
231 Adrian Road
Suite MPB
Millbrae, CA 94030

Please include 50 cents for postage and handling.
California residents add 6% tax.